# Magnificent Mandalas

Designs to Inspire Your Creative Genius

Published in 2015 by Global Insight Productions

Illustrated by Lyric Libretto
and some Images used under license from Shutterstock.com

www.BeHappyColoringBooks.com

ISBN: 9780979694257

# Join Our Creative Community

## BeHappyColoringBooks.com

For your coloring and painting pleasure,
if you have creative genius ideas that you
would like for our artist to design, let us know.

We also want you to be a part of our Be Happy
Art Gallery. So go ahead and send us your
masterpiece and we will share it with the world.

You can contact us at **info@behappycoloring.com**

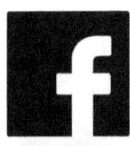 facebook.com/behappycoloring

 pinterest.com/behappycoloring

 Instagram.com/behappycoloring

 twitter.com/behappycoloring

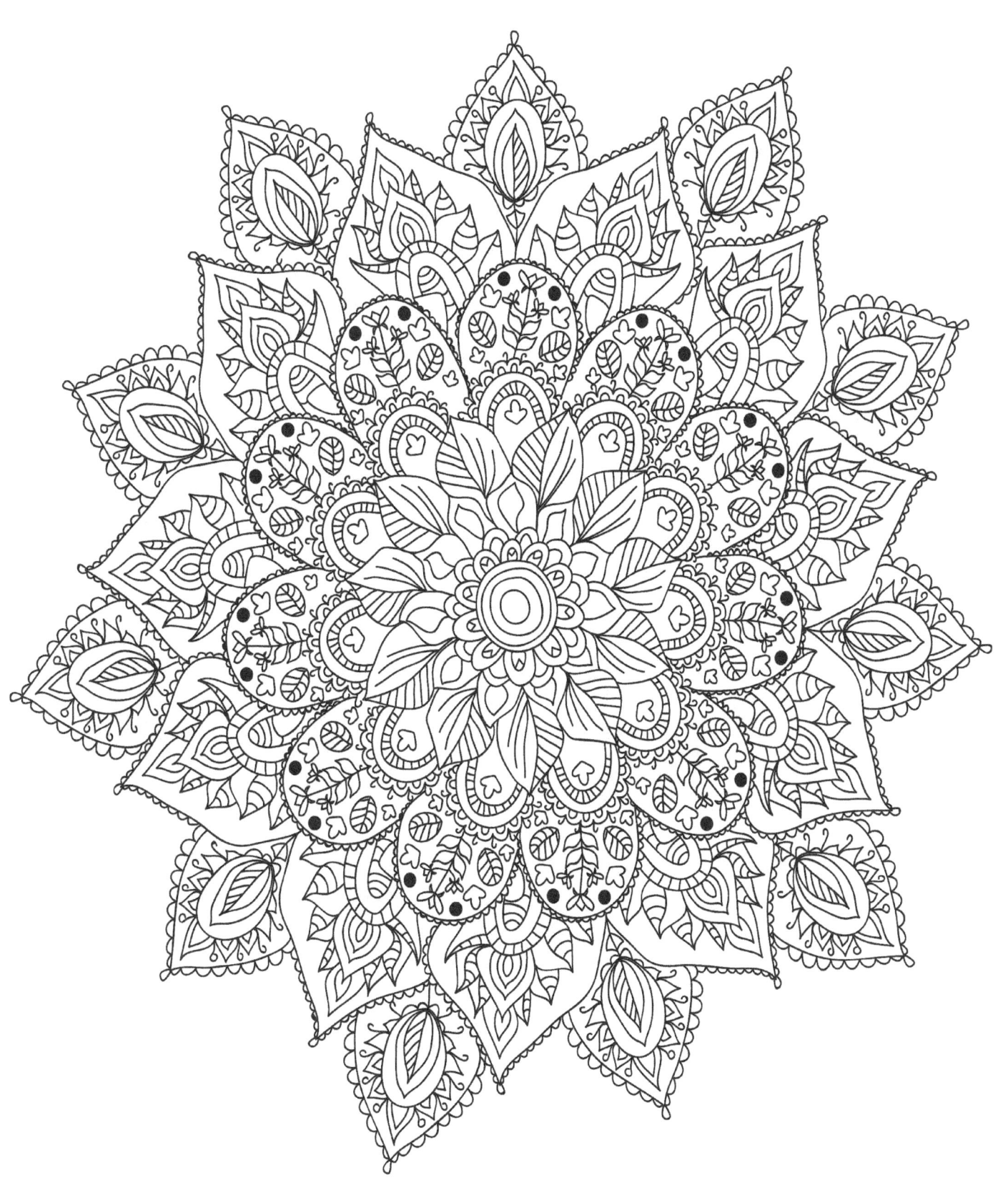

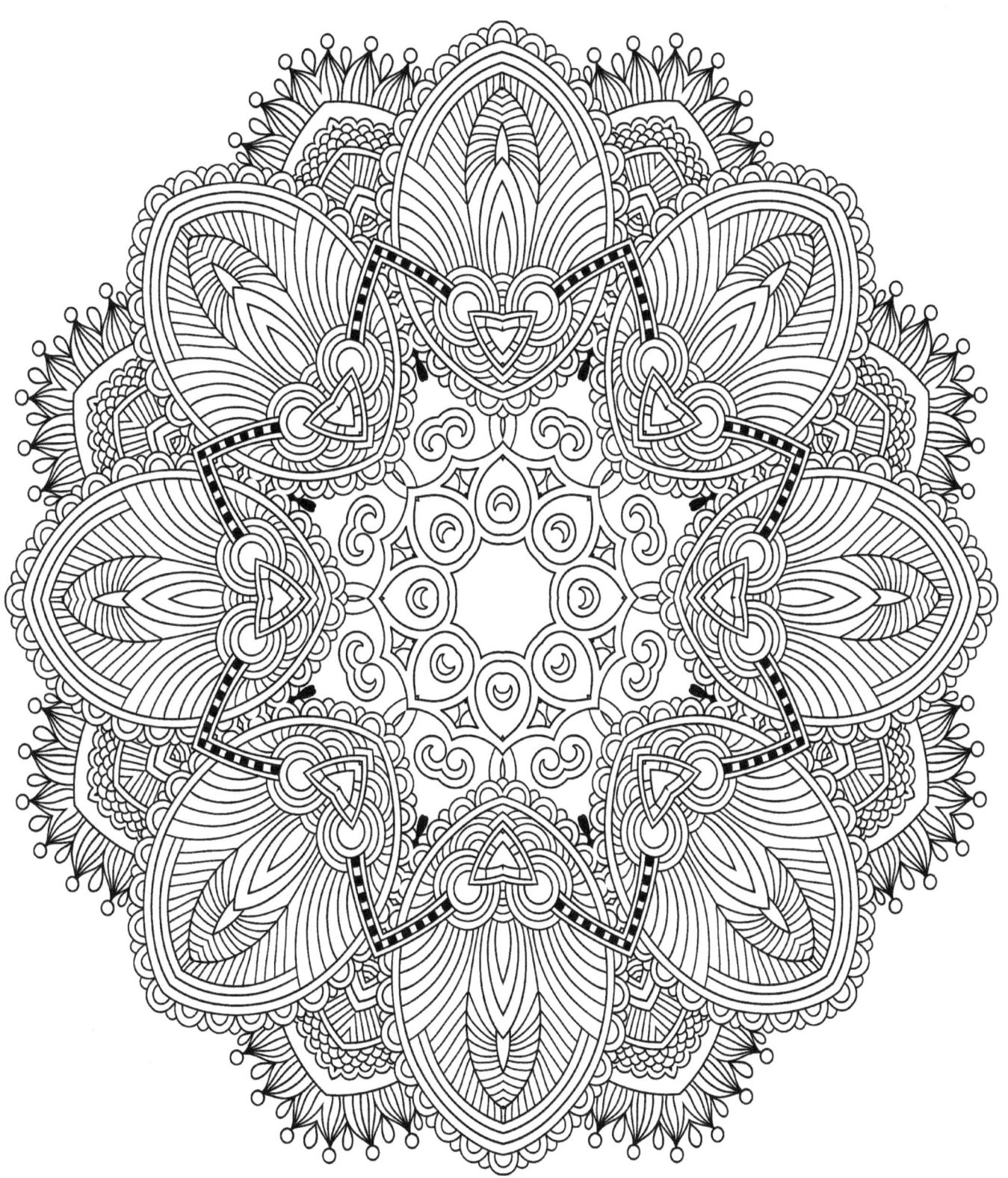

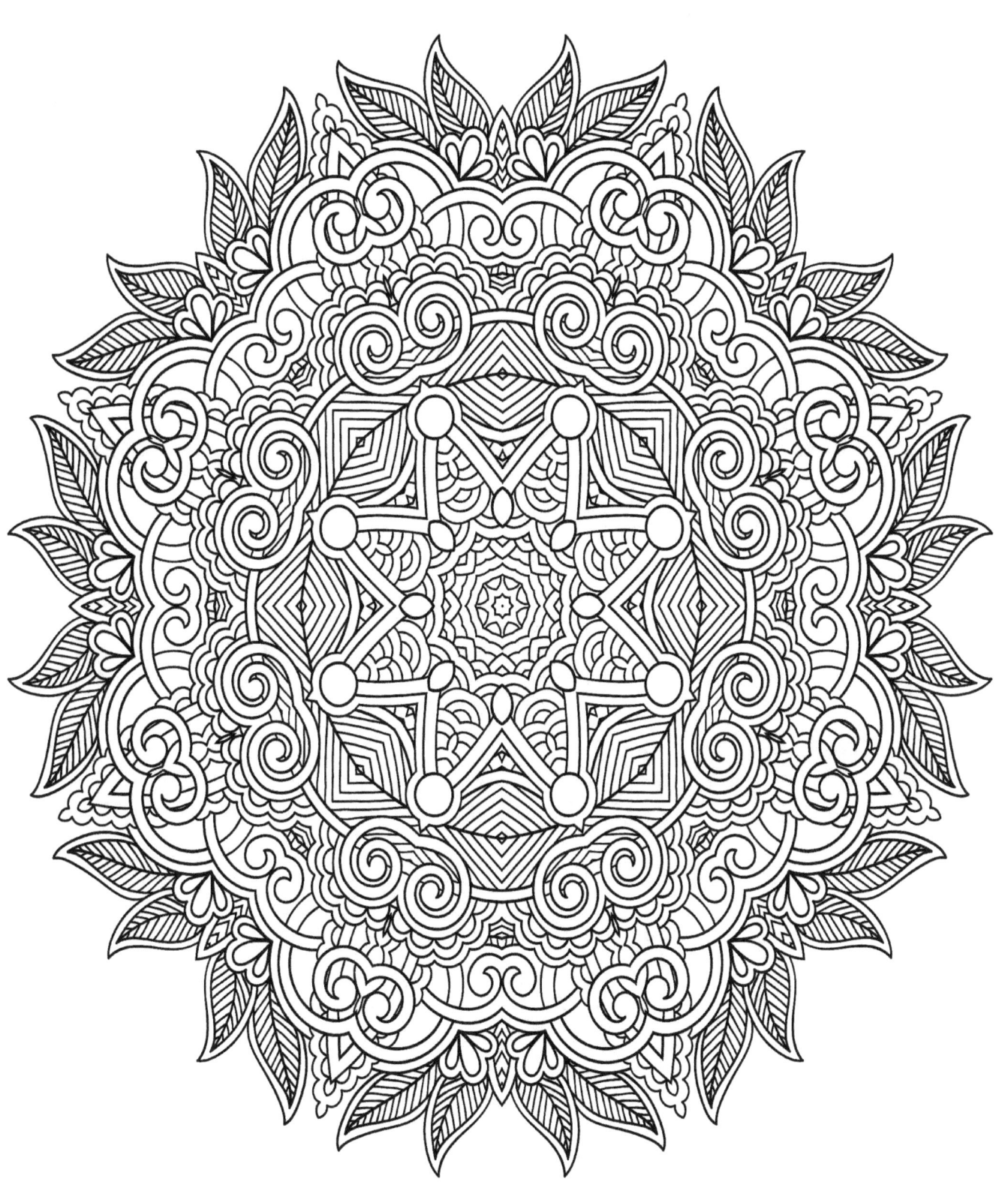

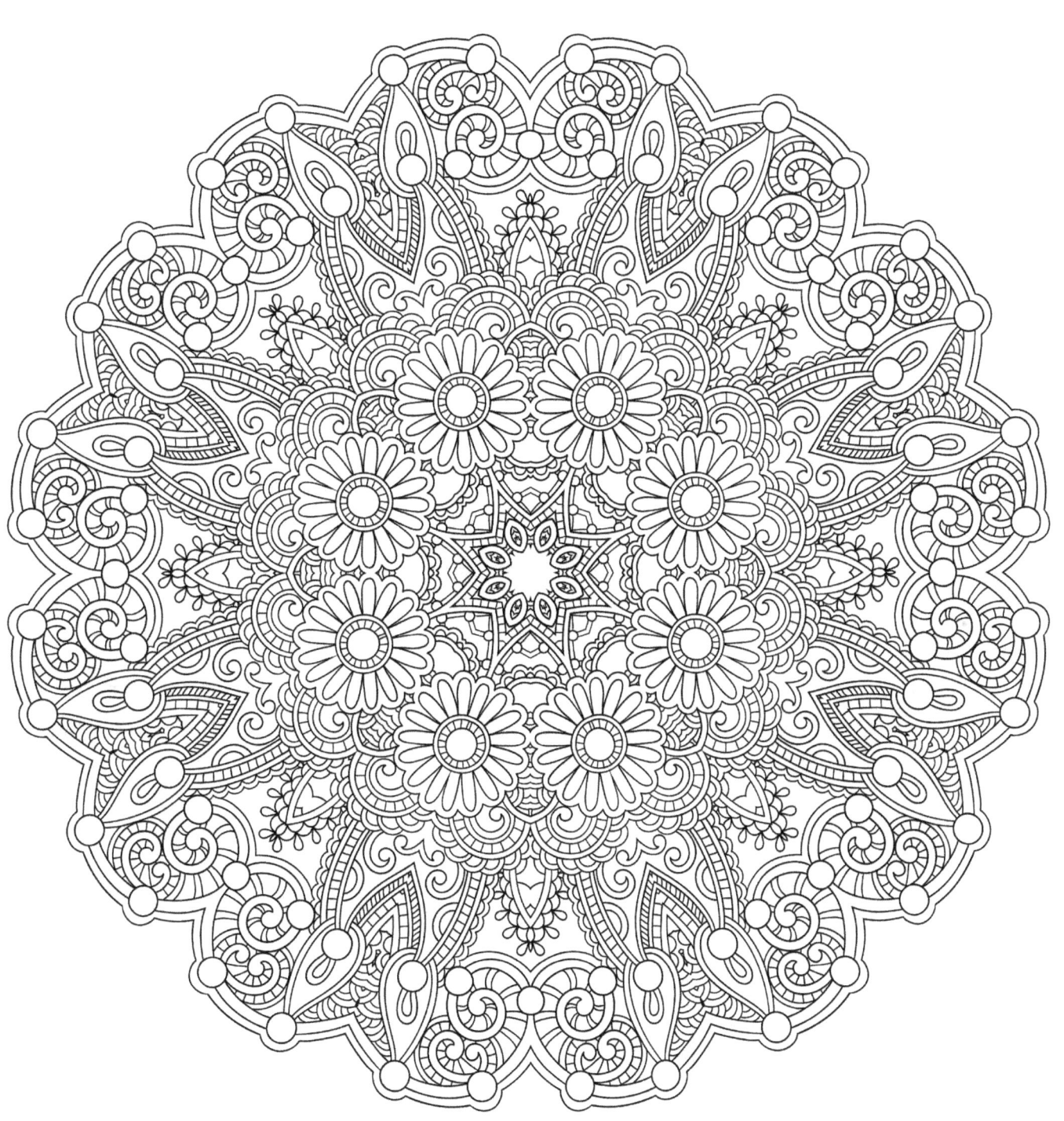

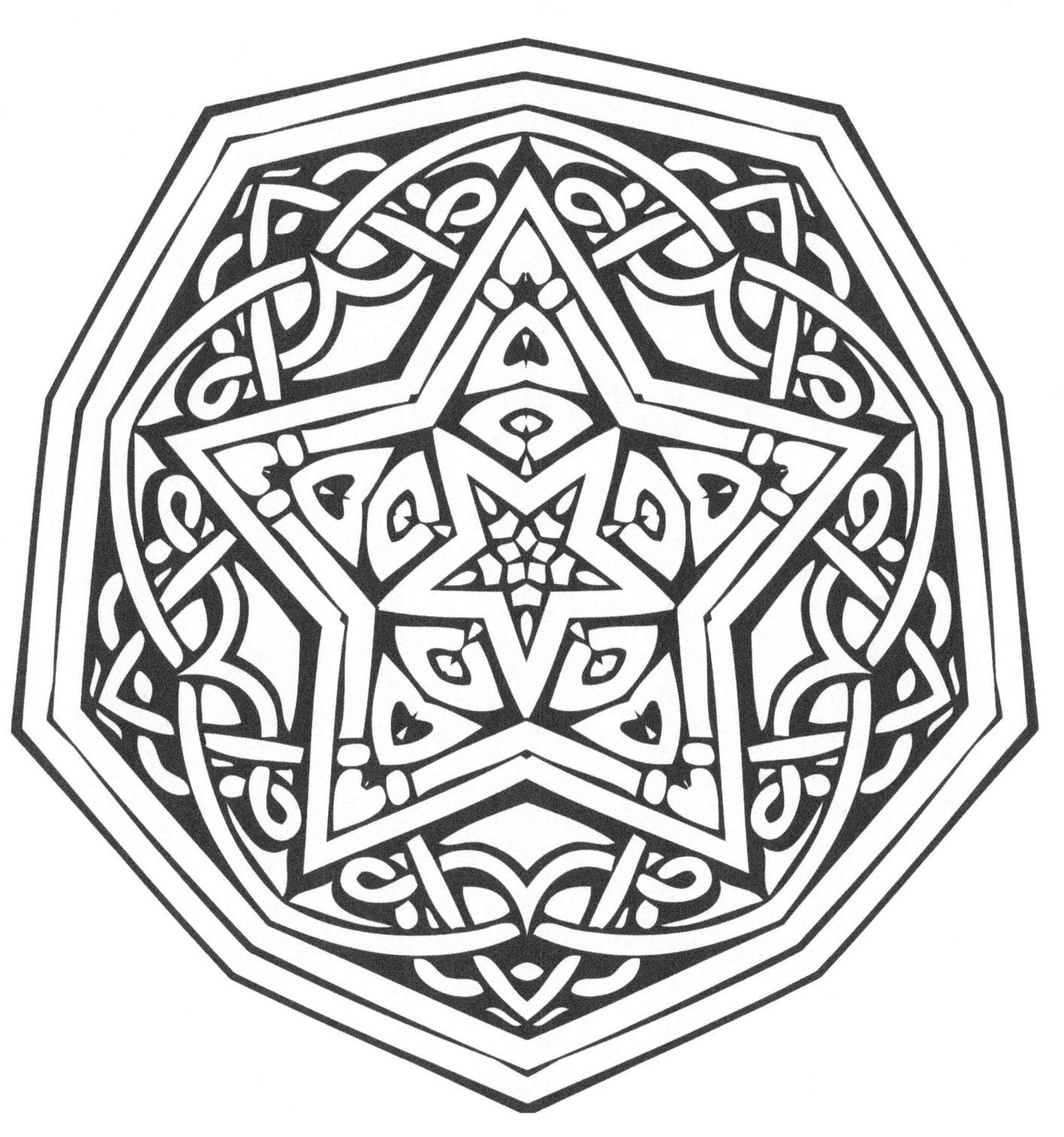

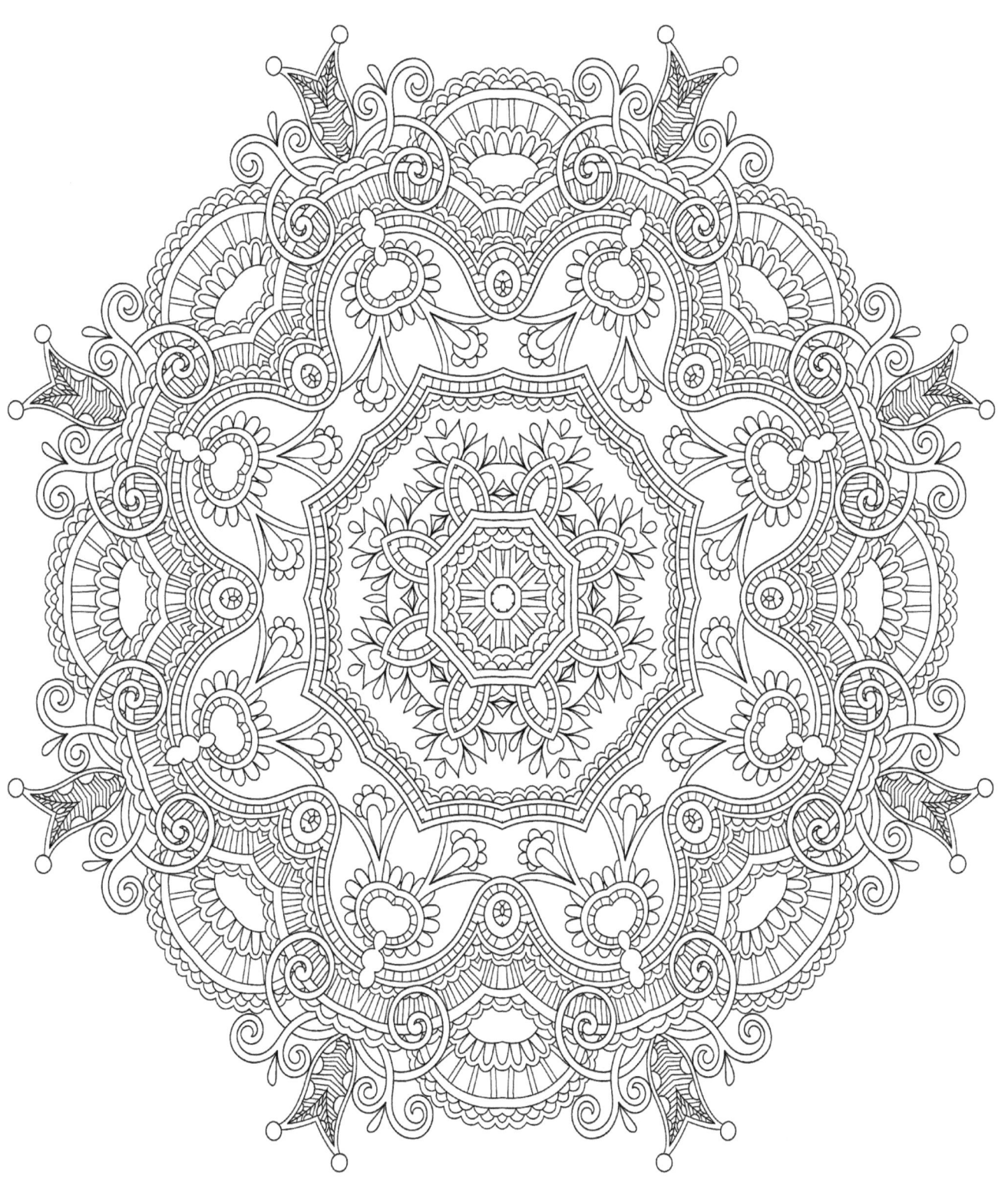

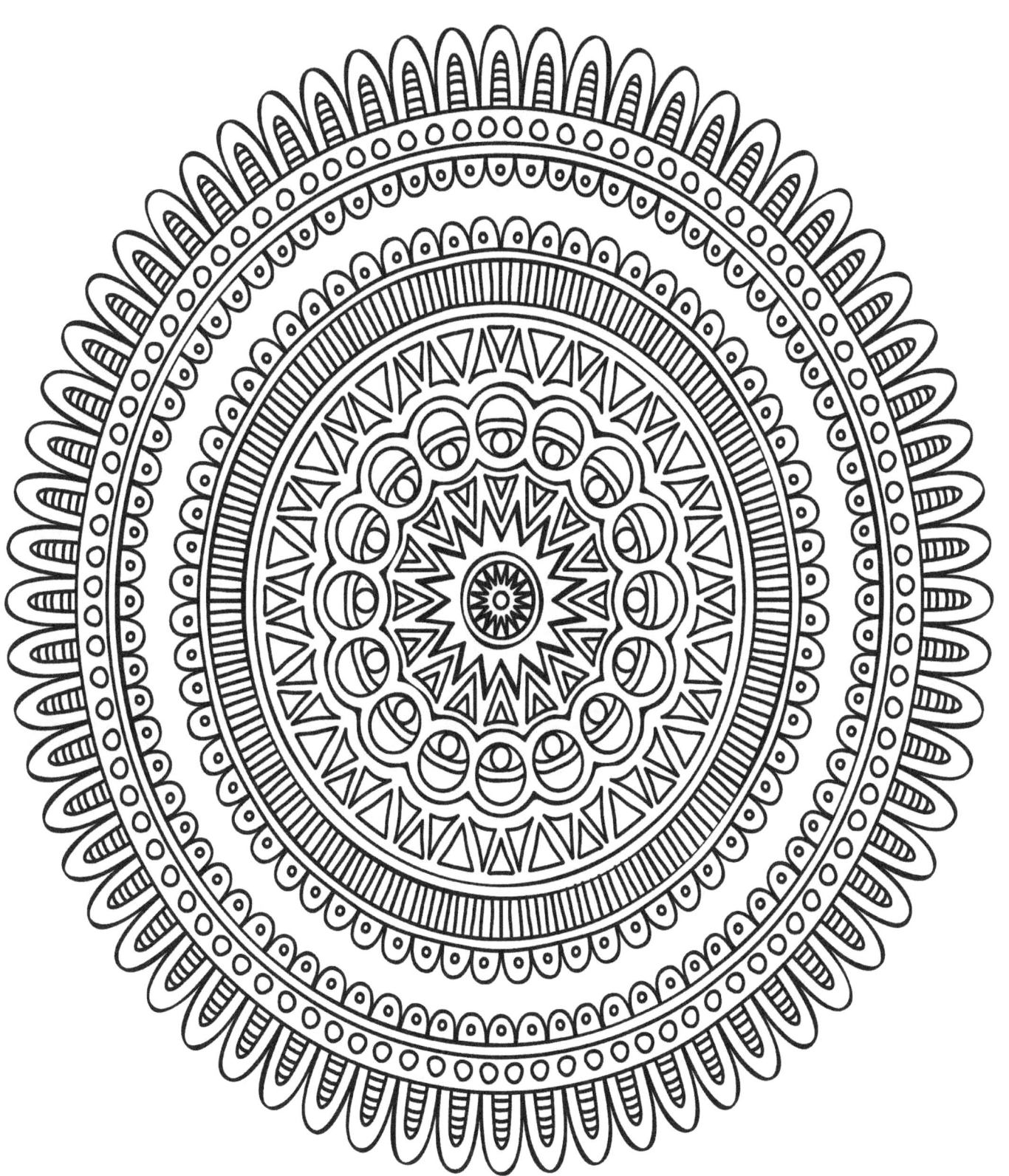

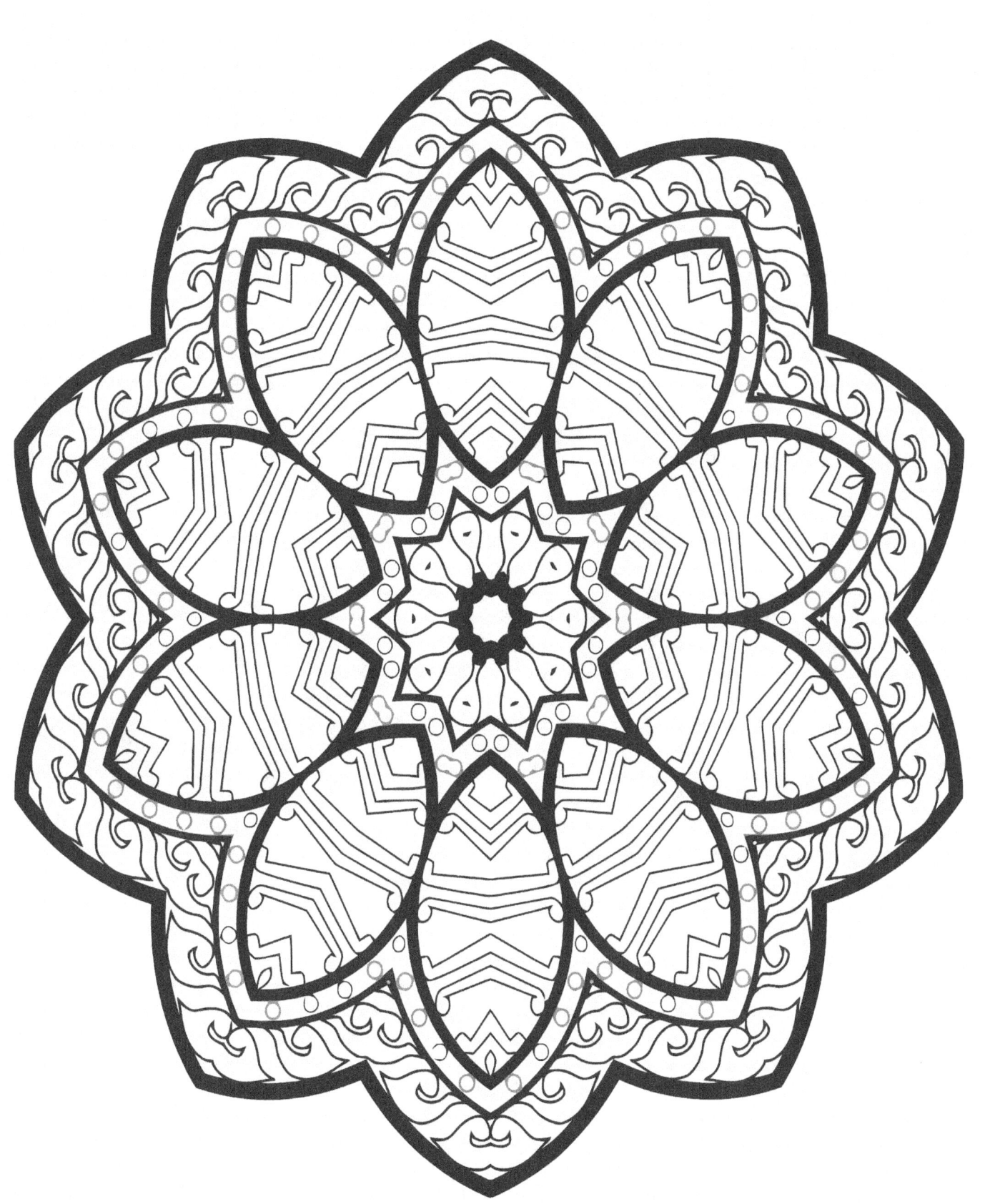

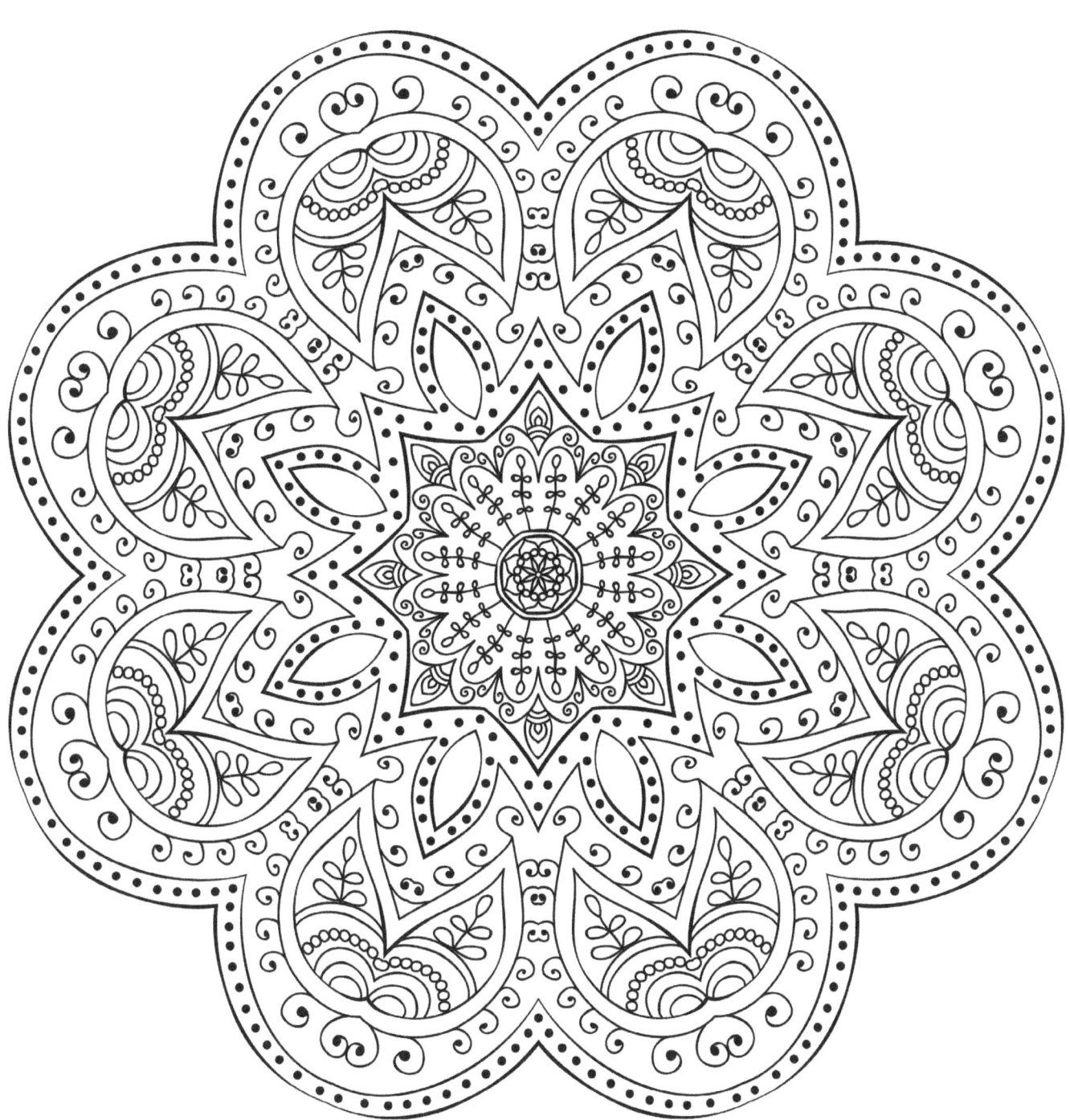

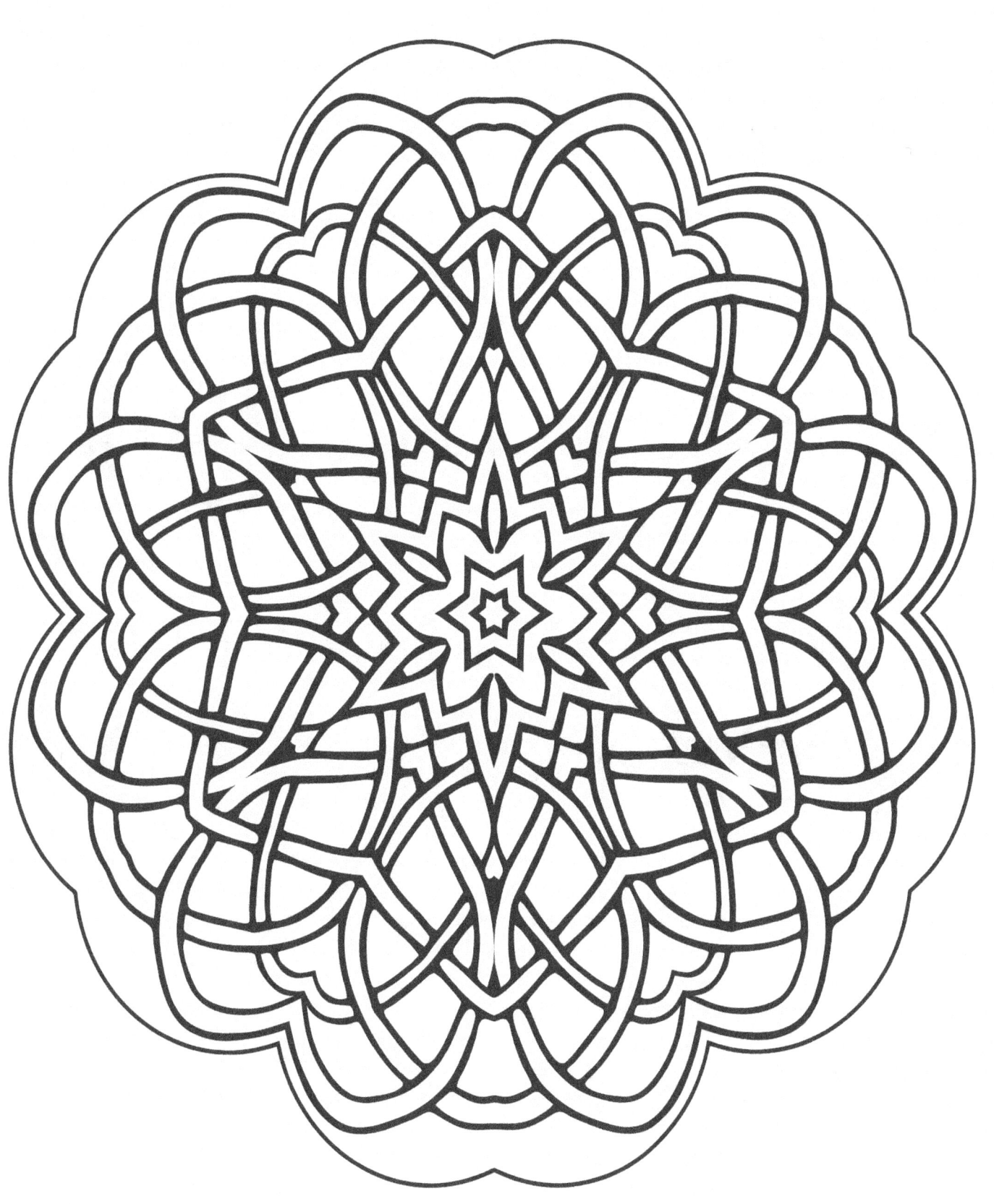

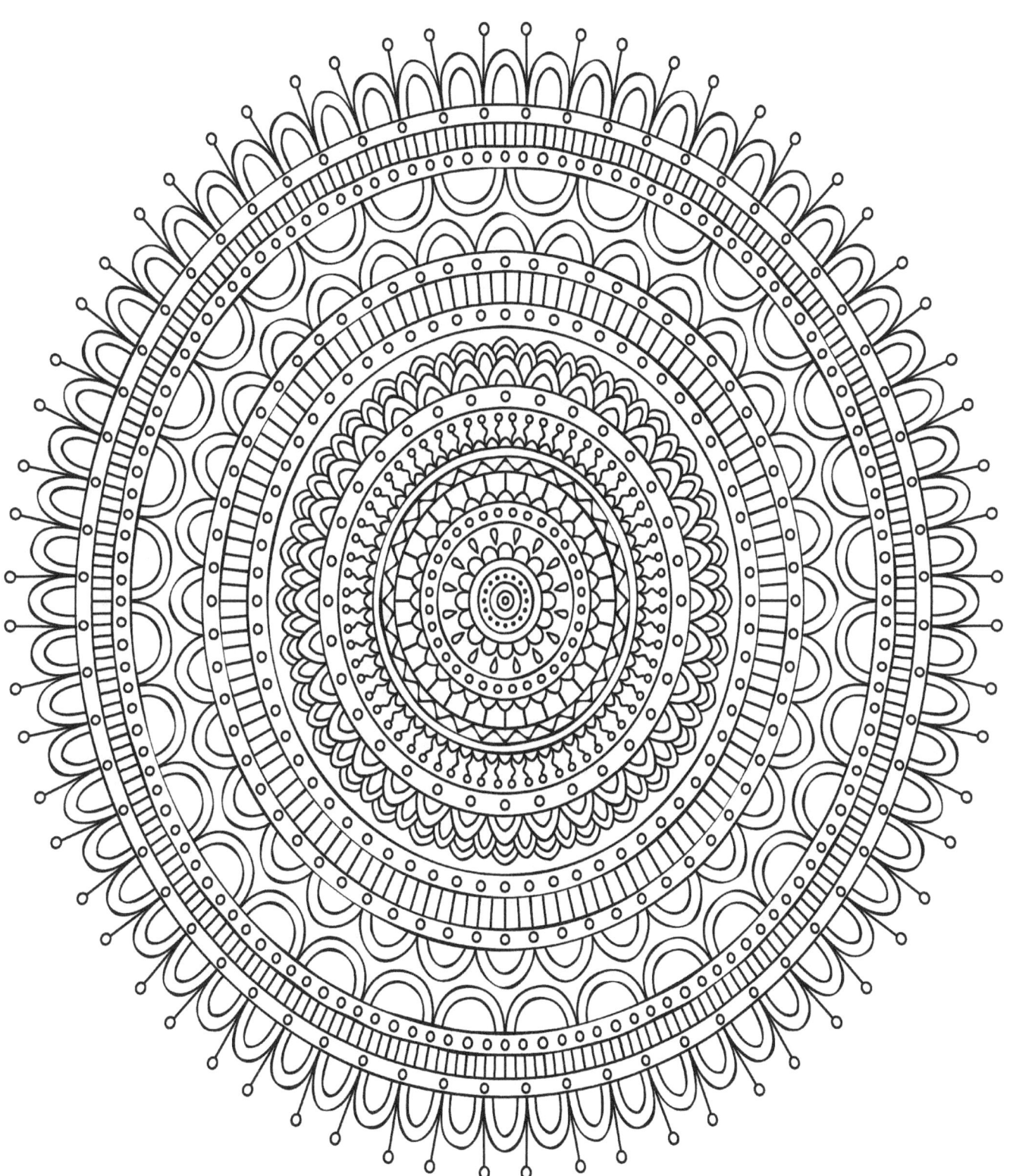

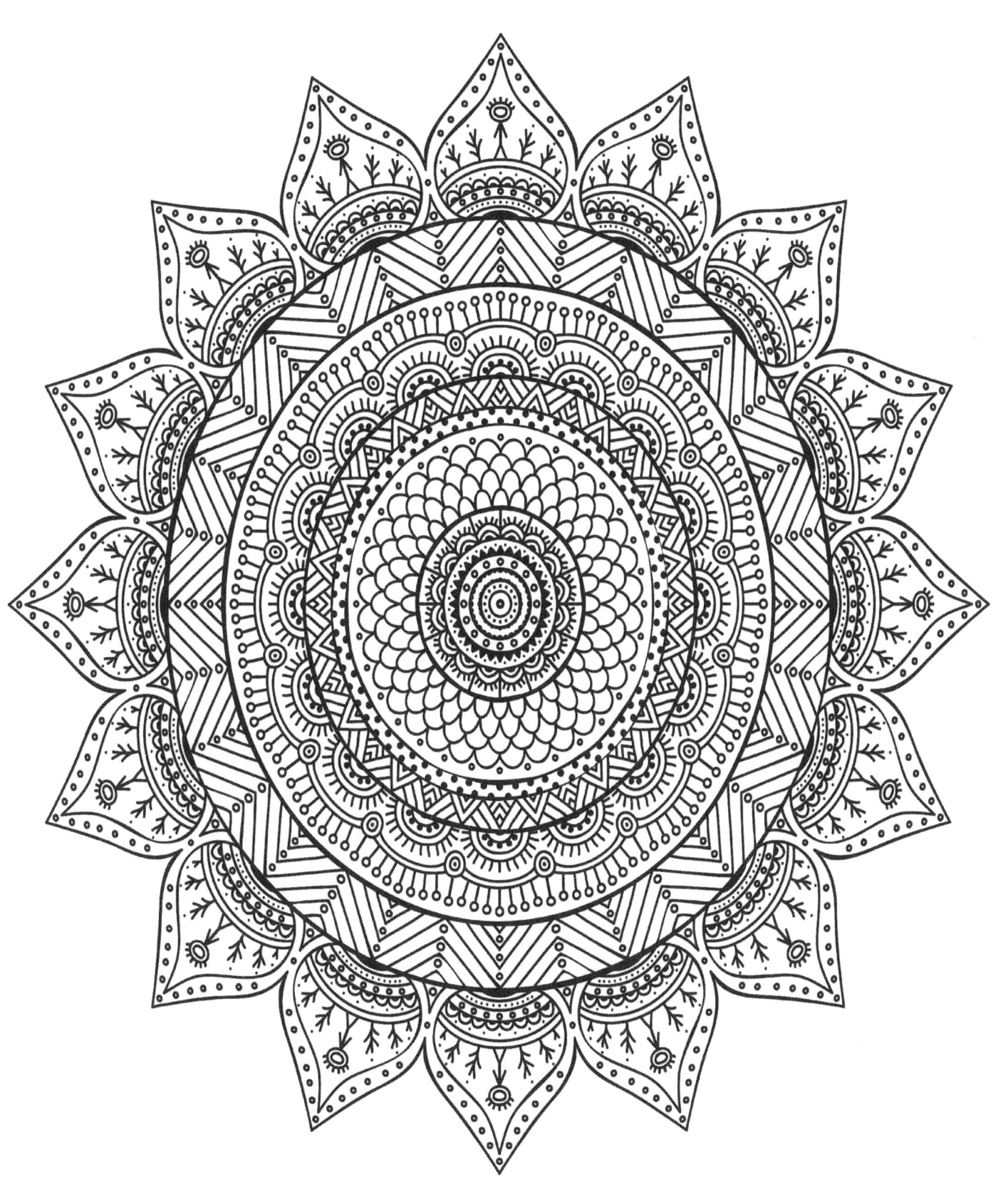

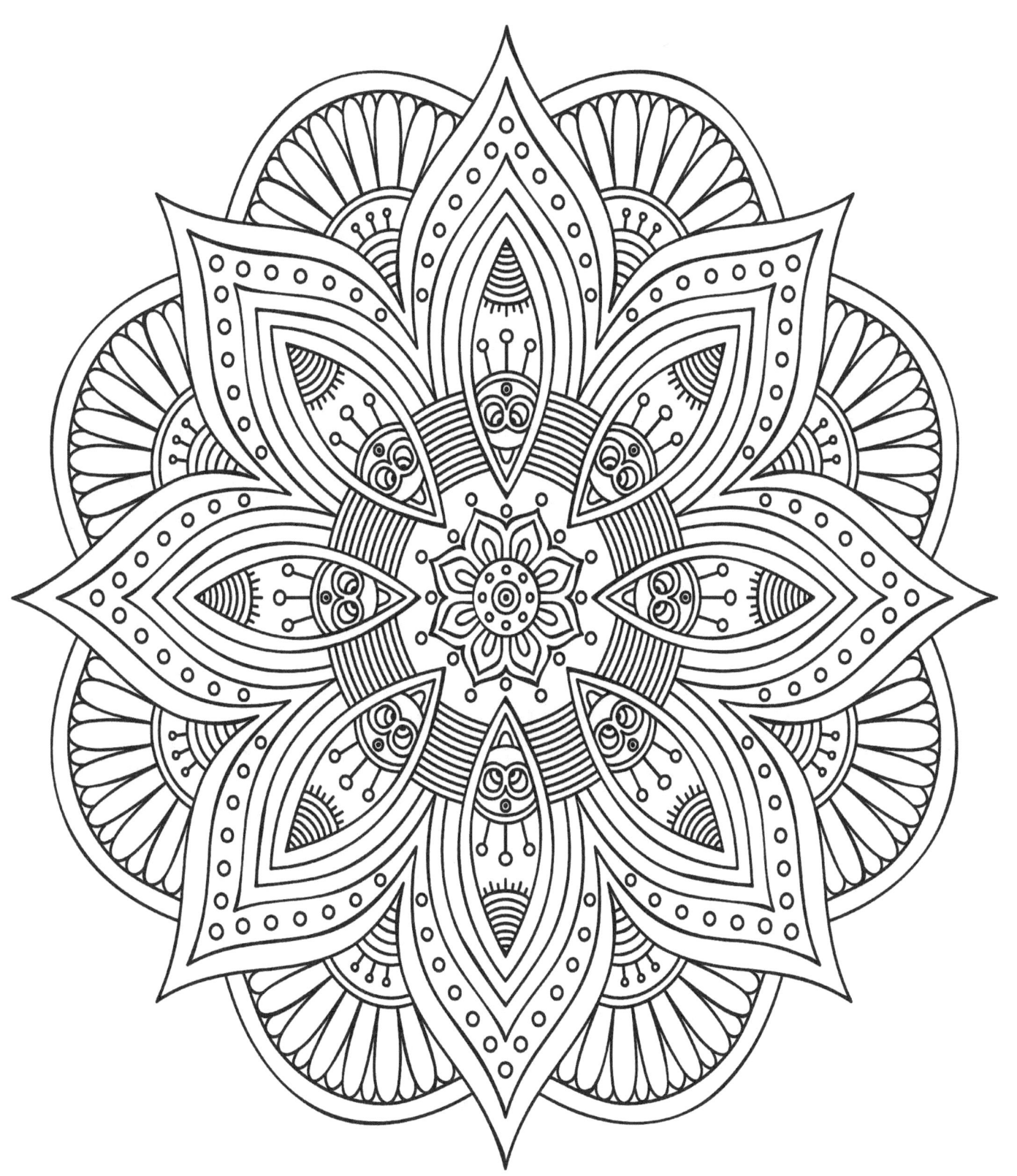

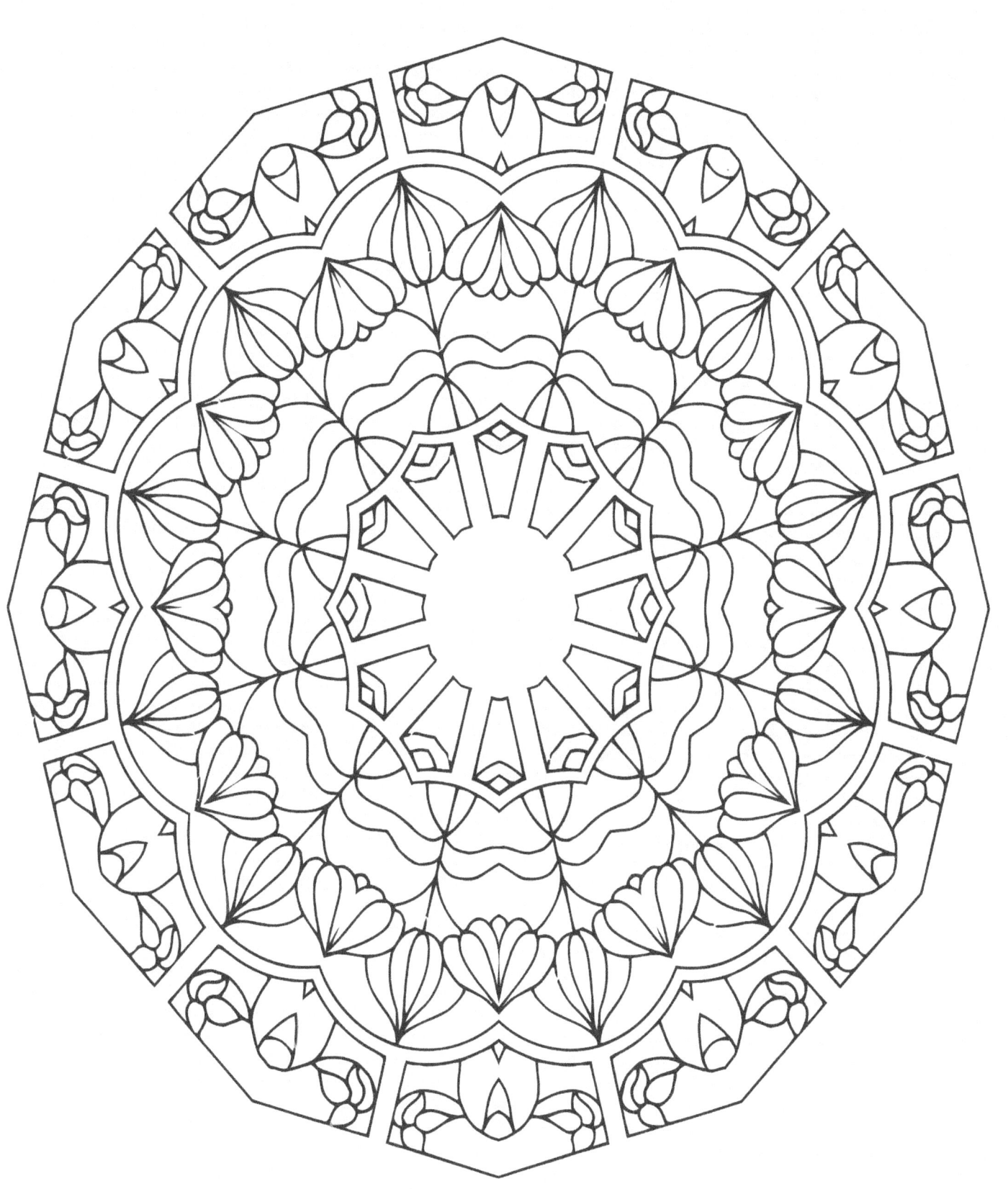

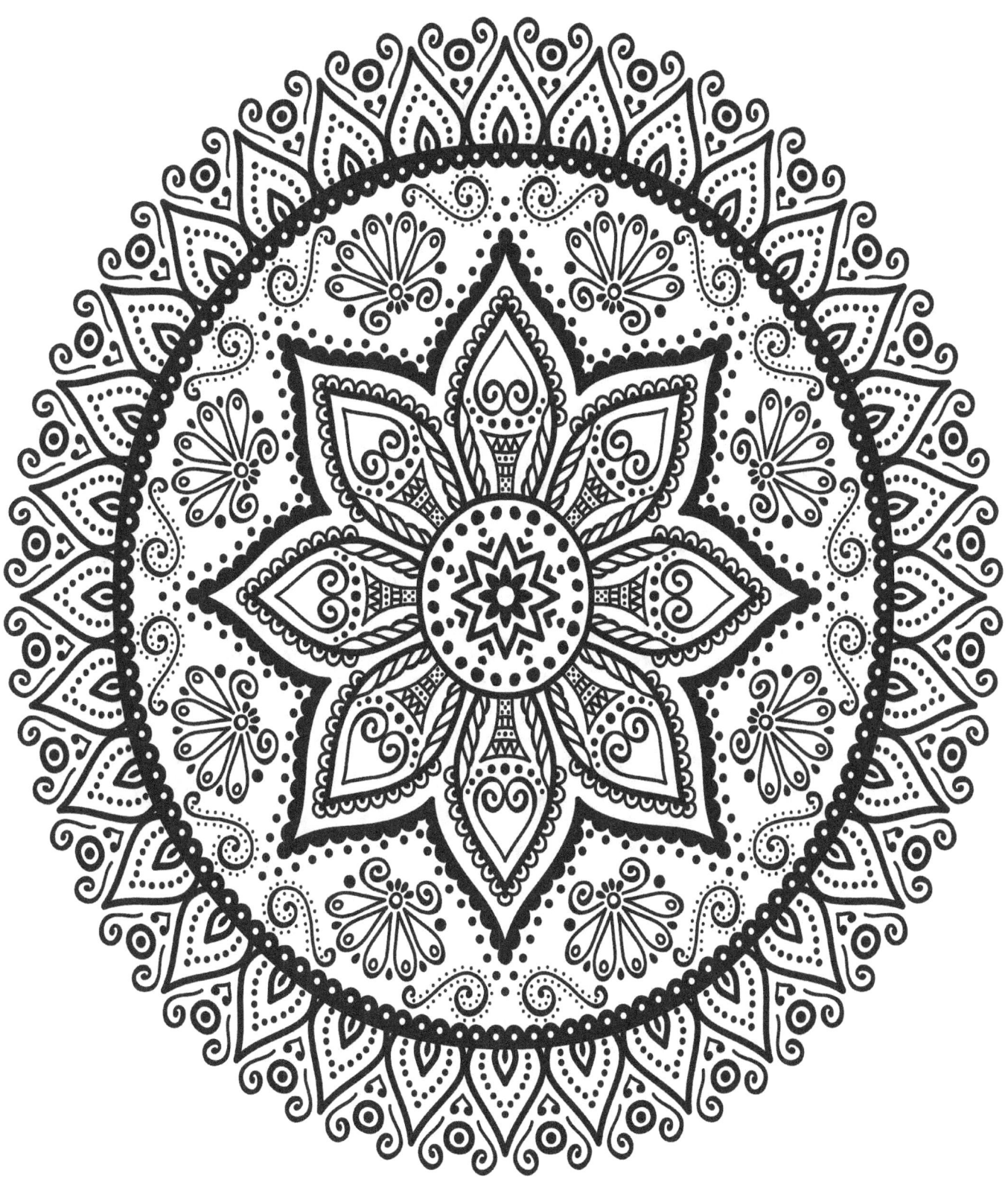

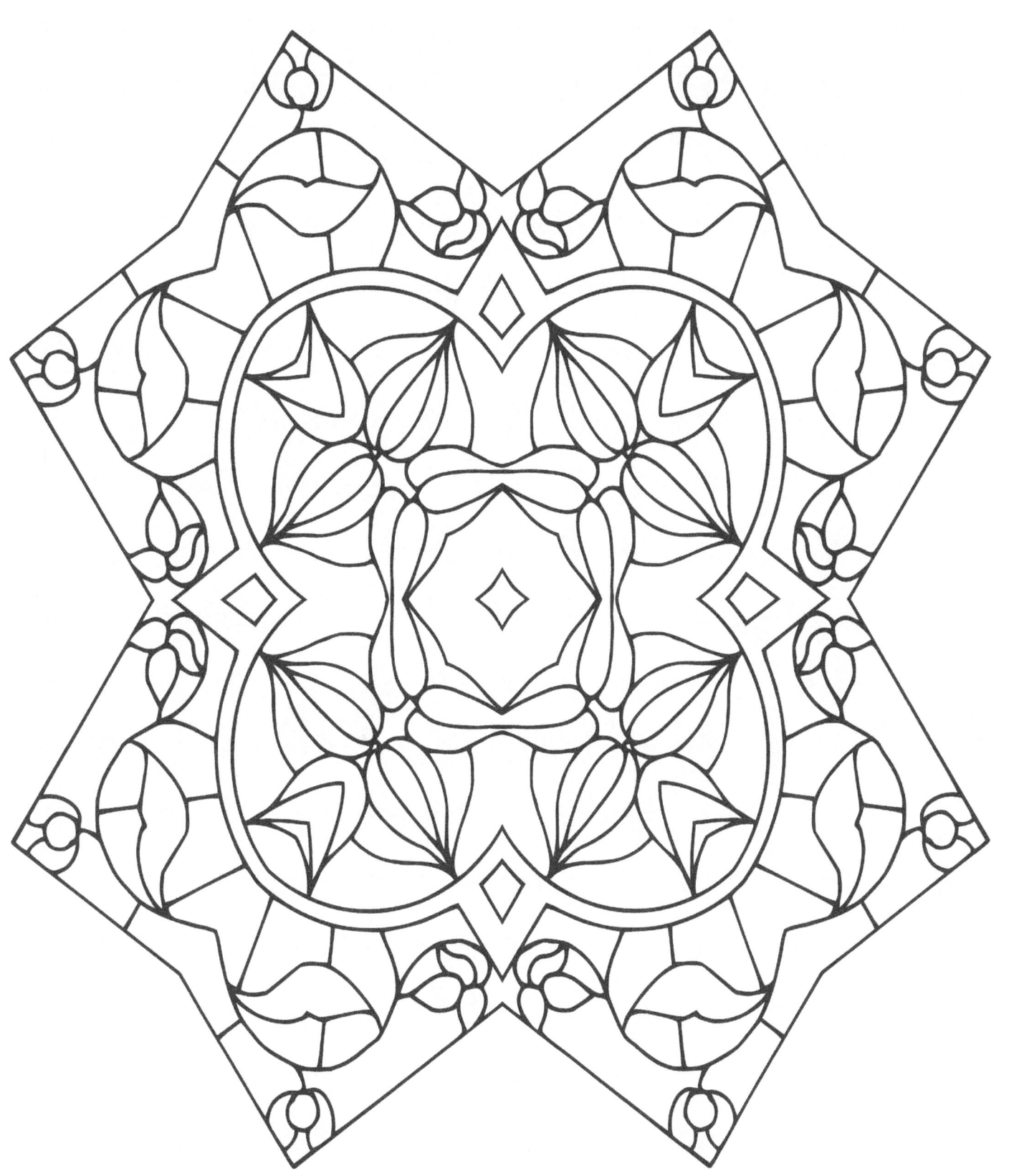

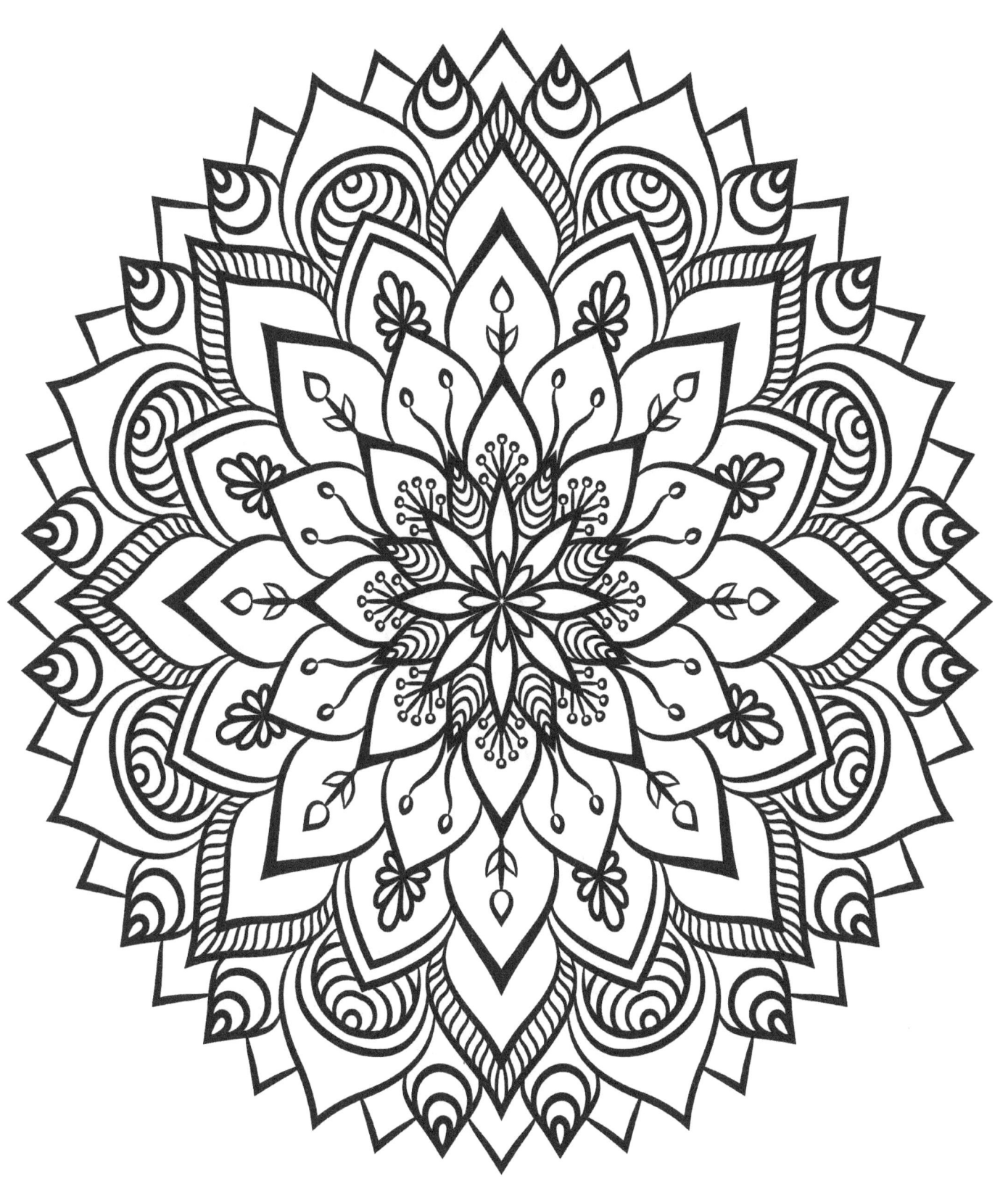

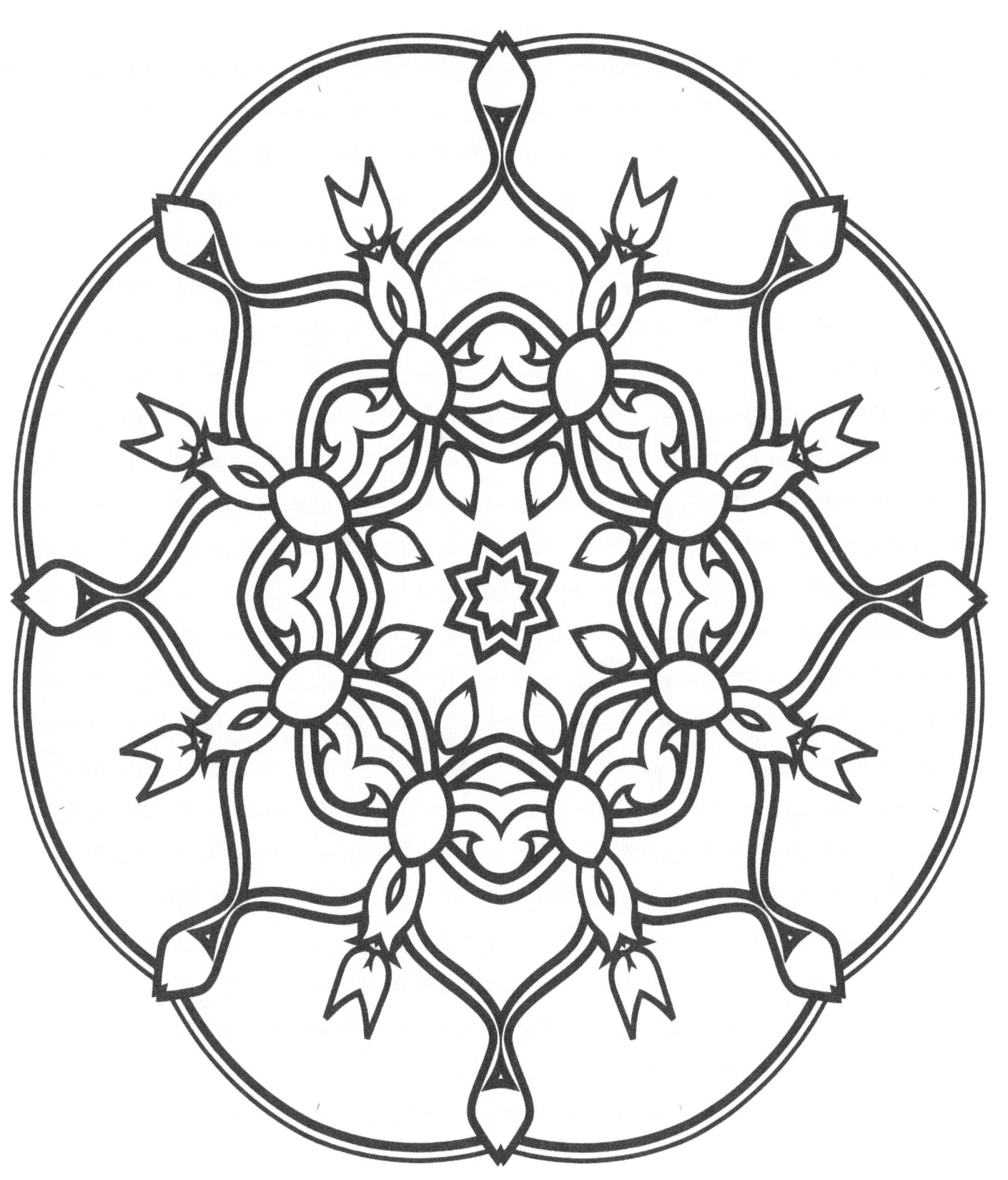

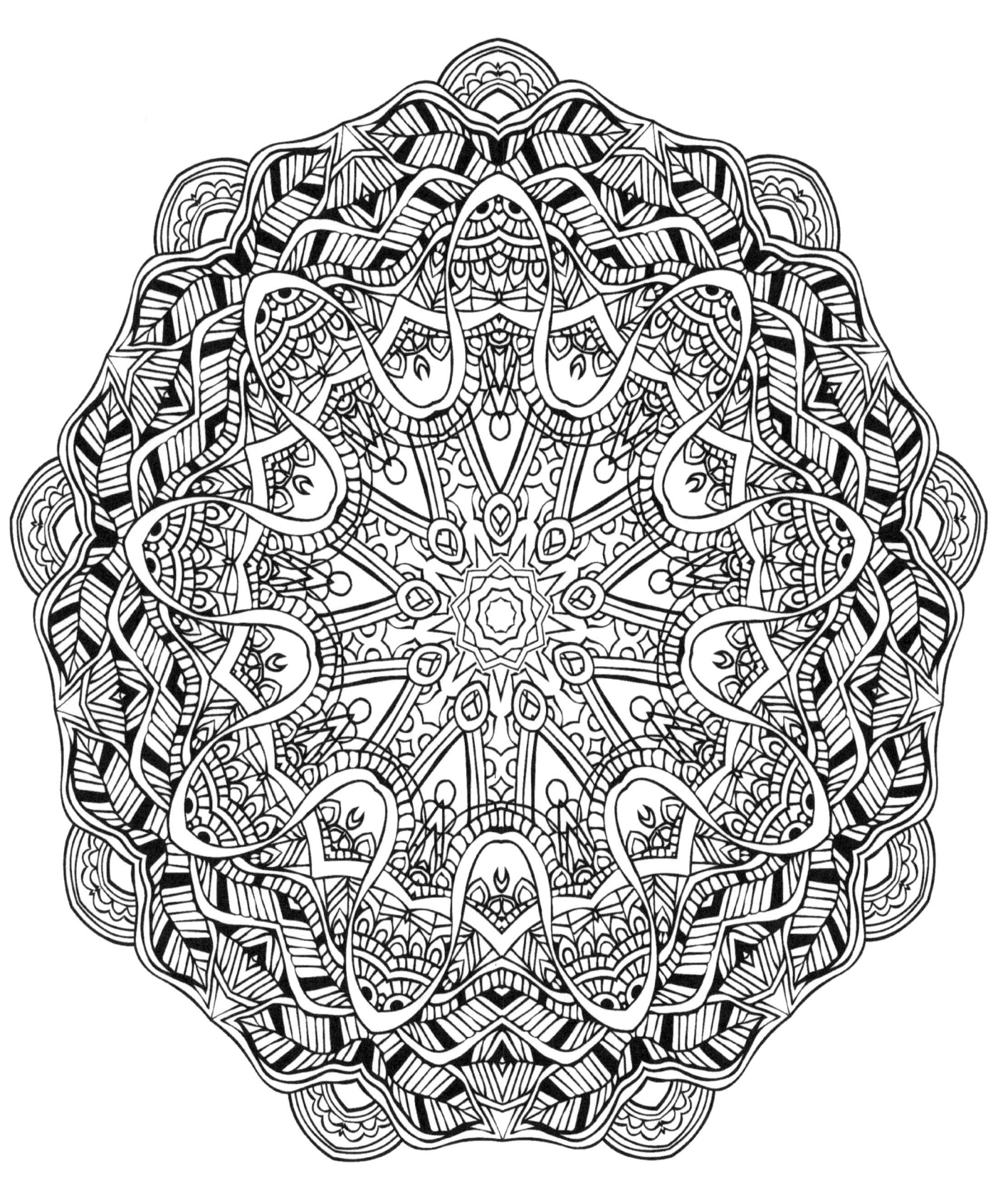

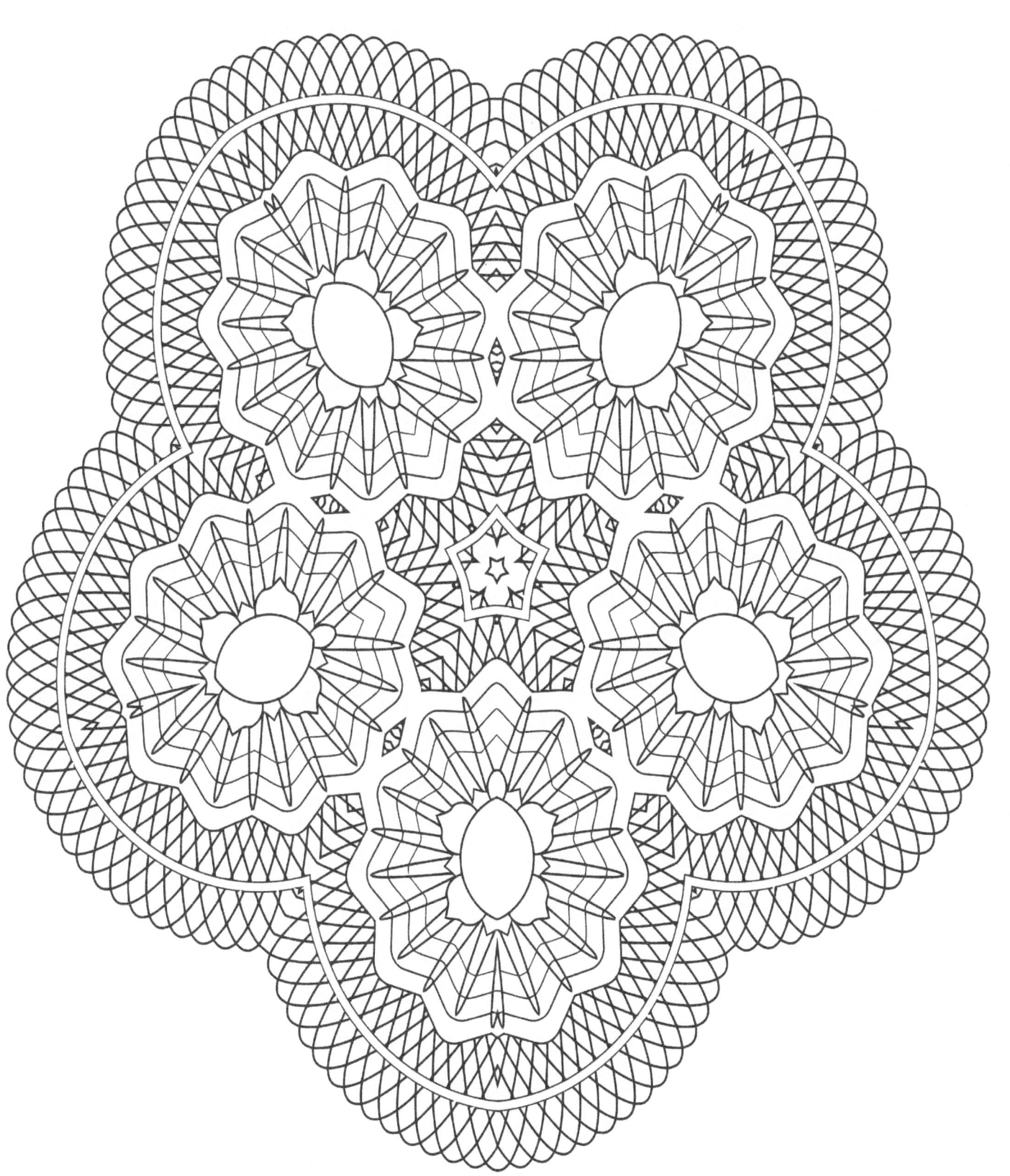

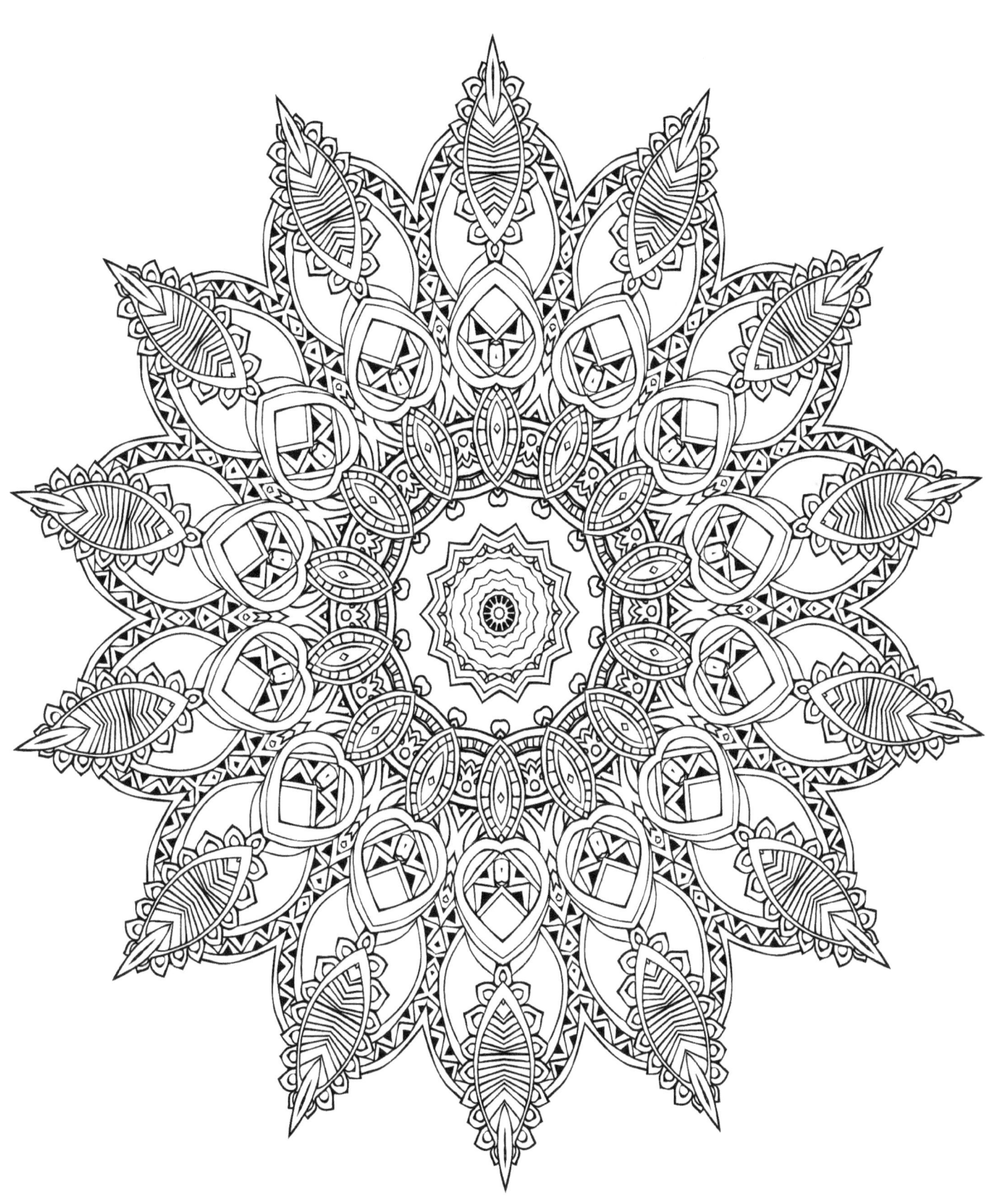

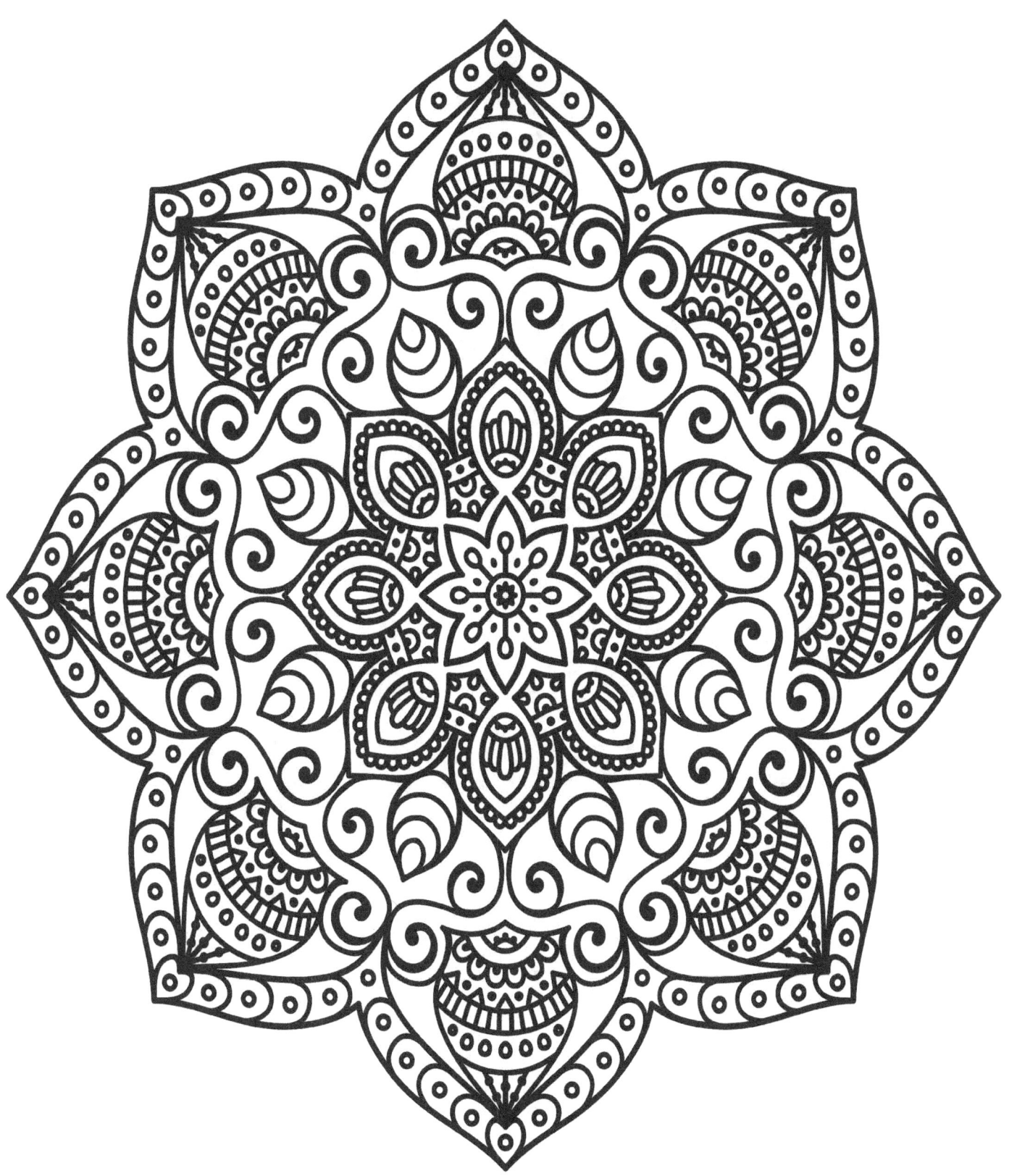

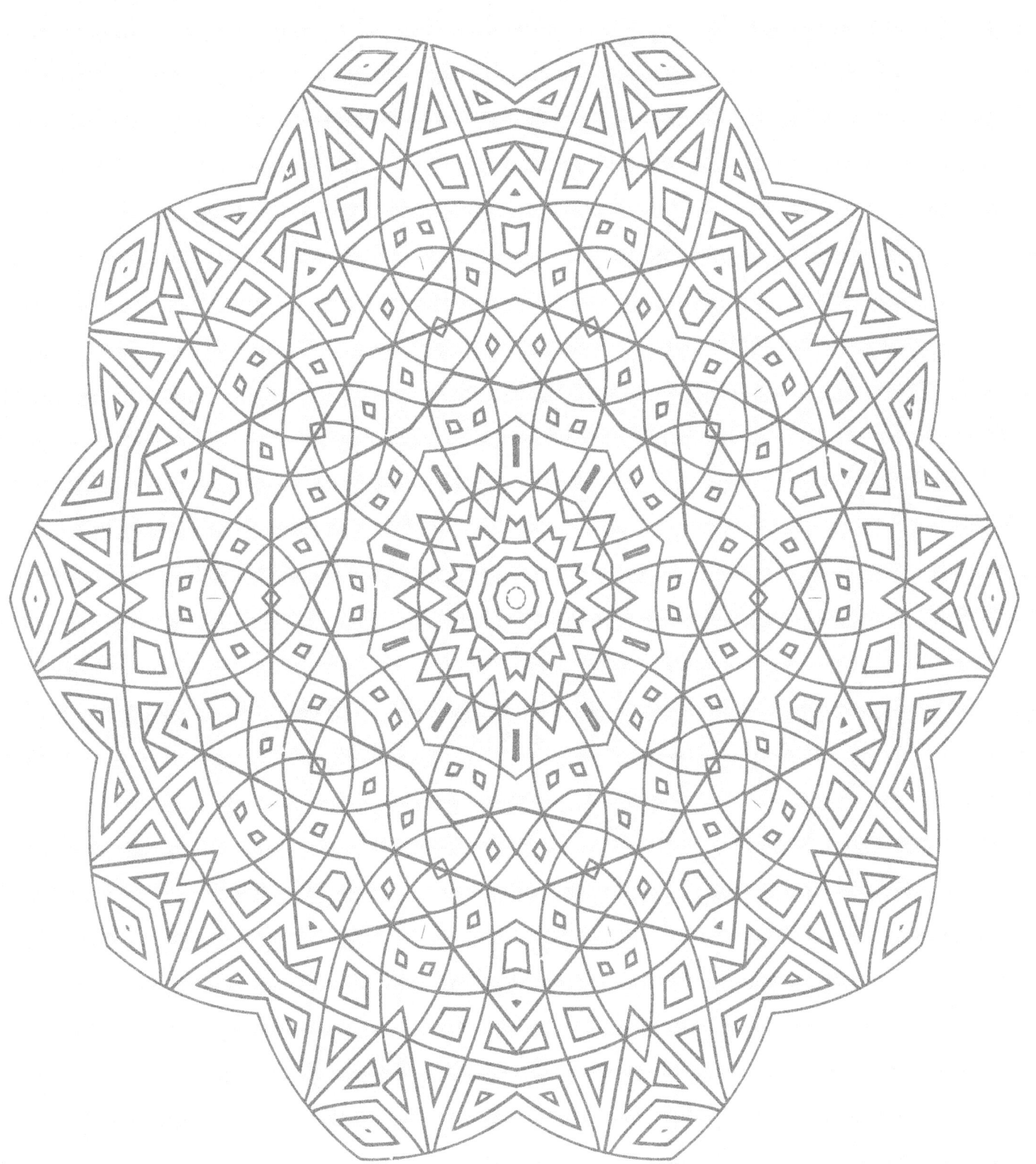

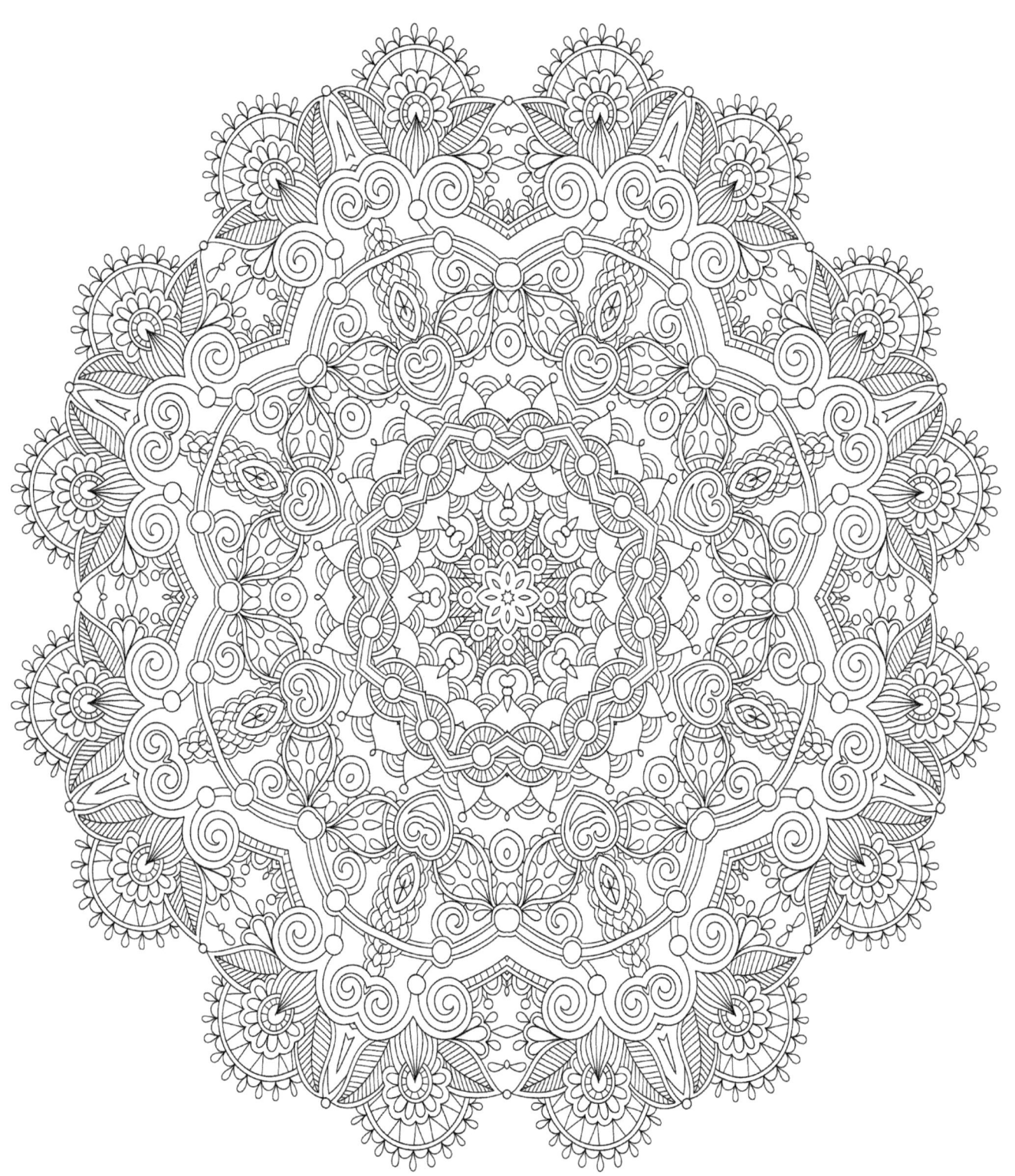

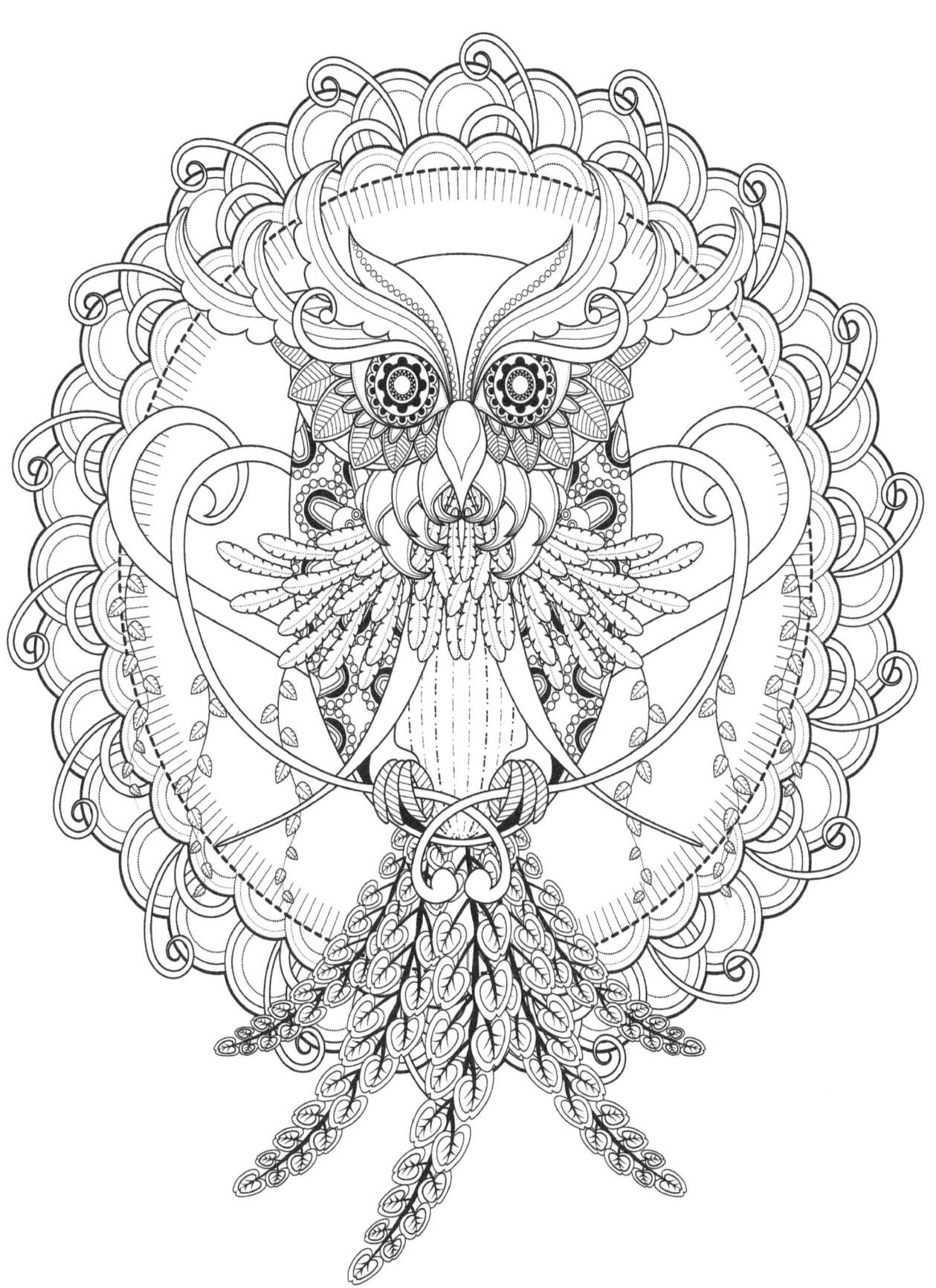

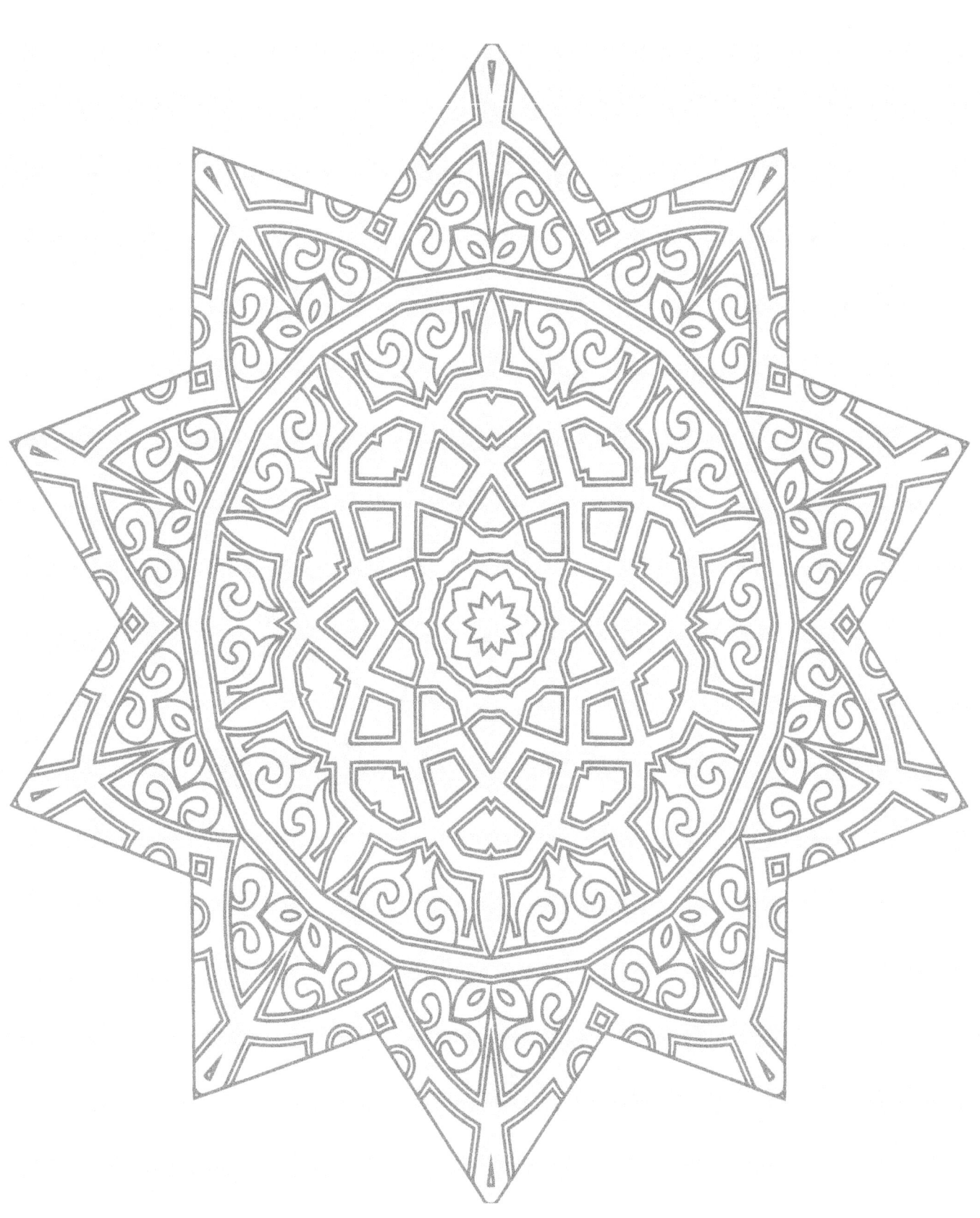

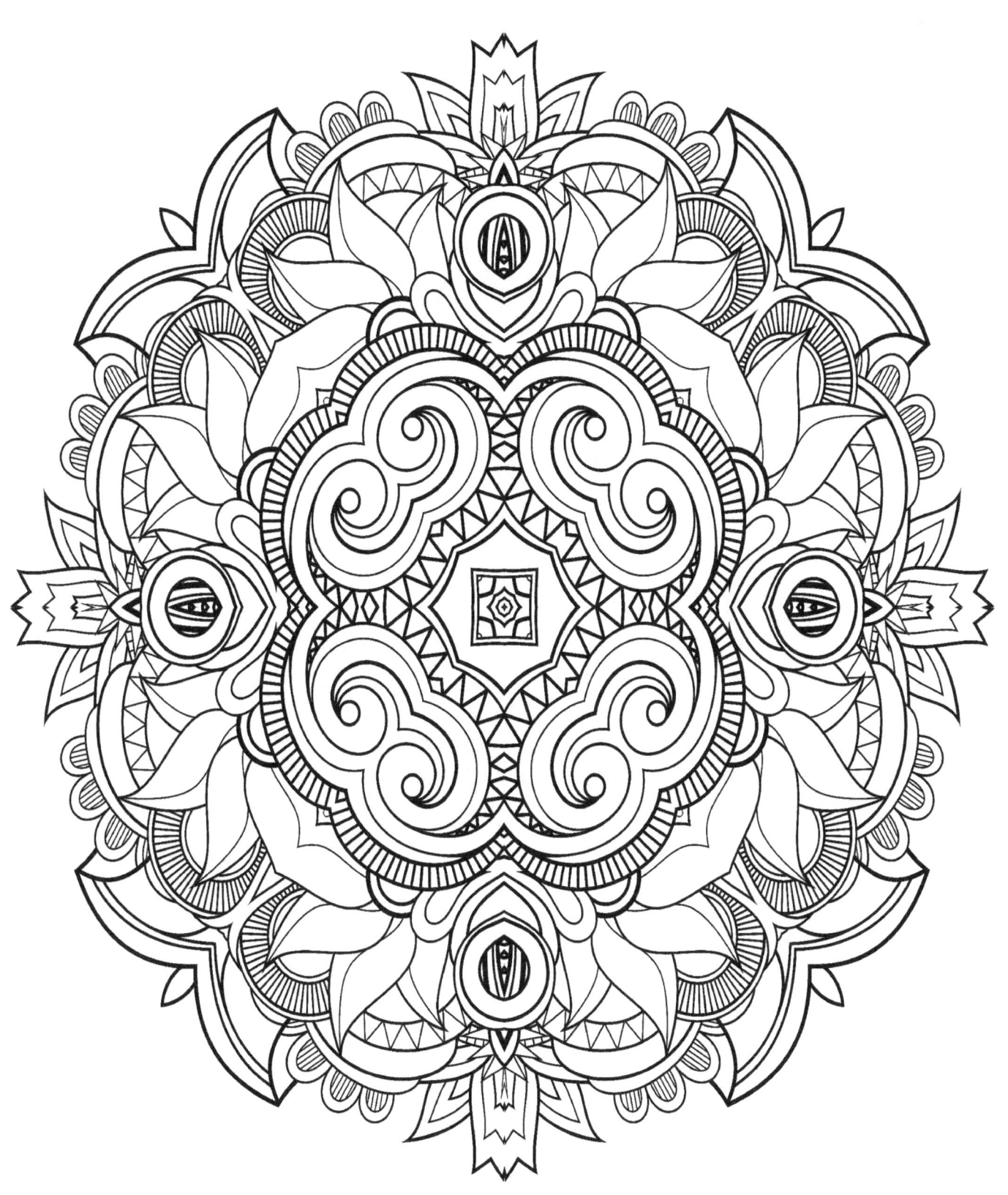

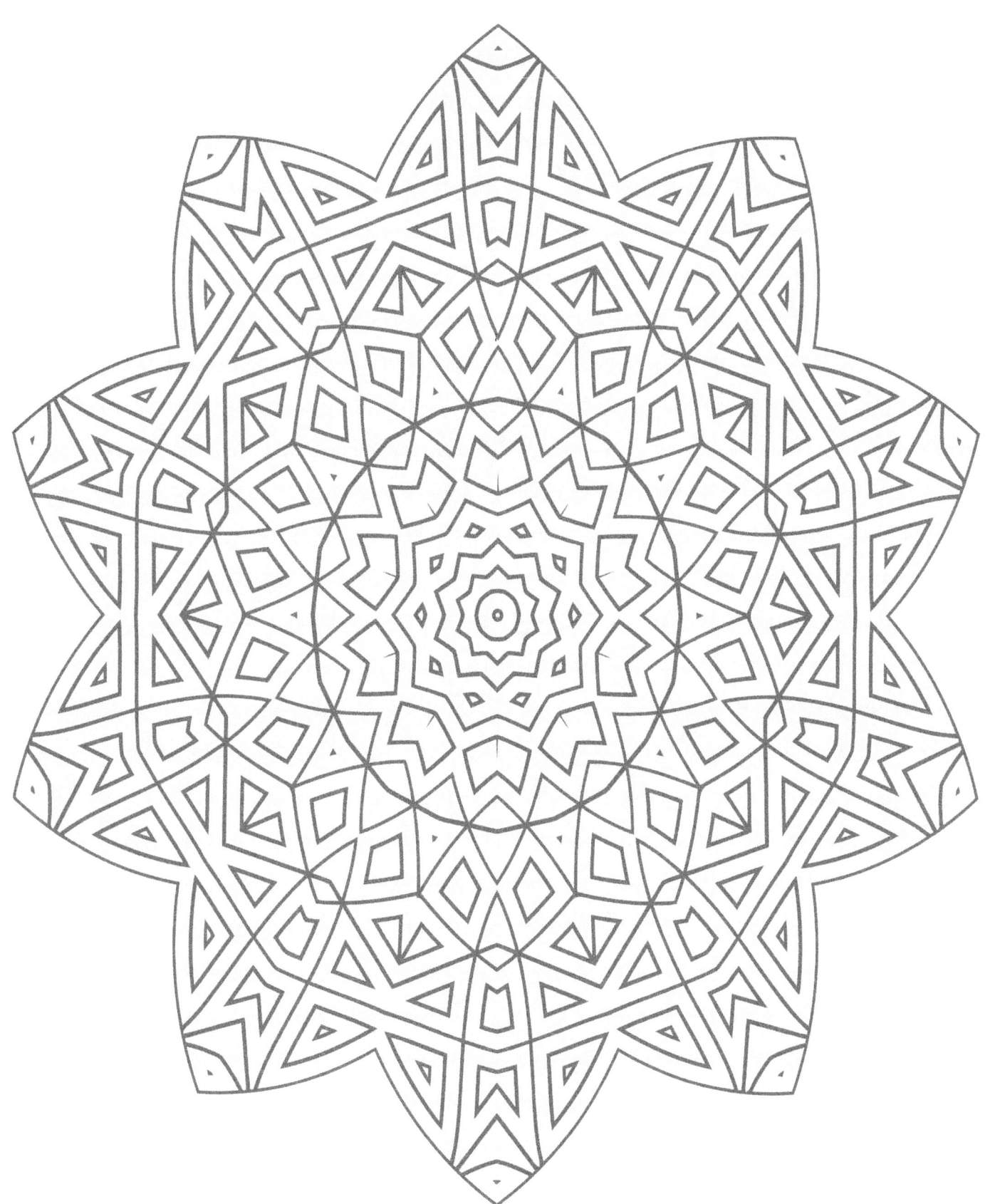

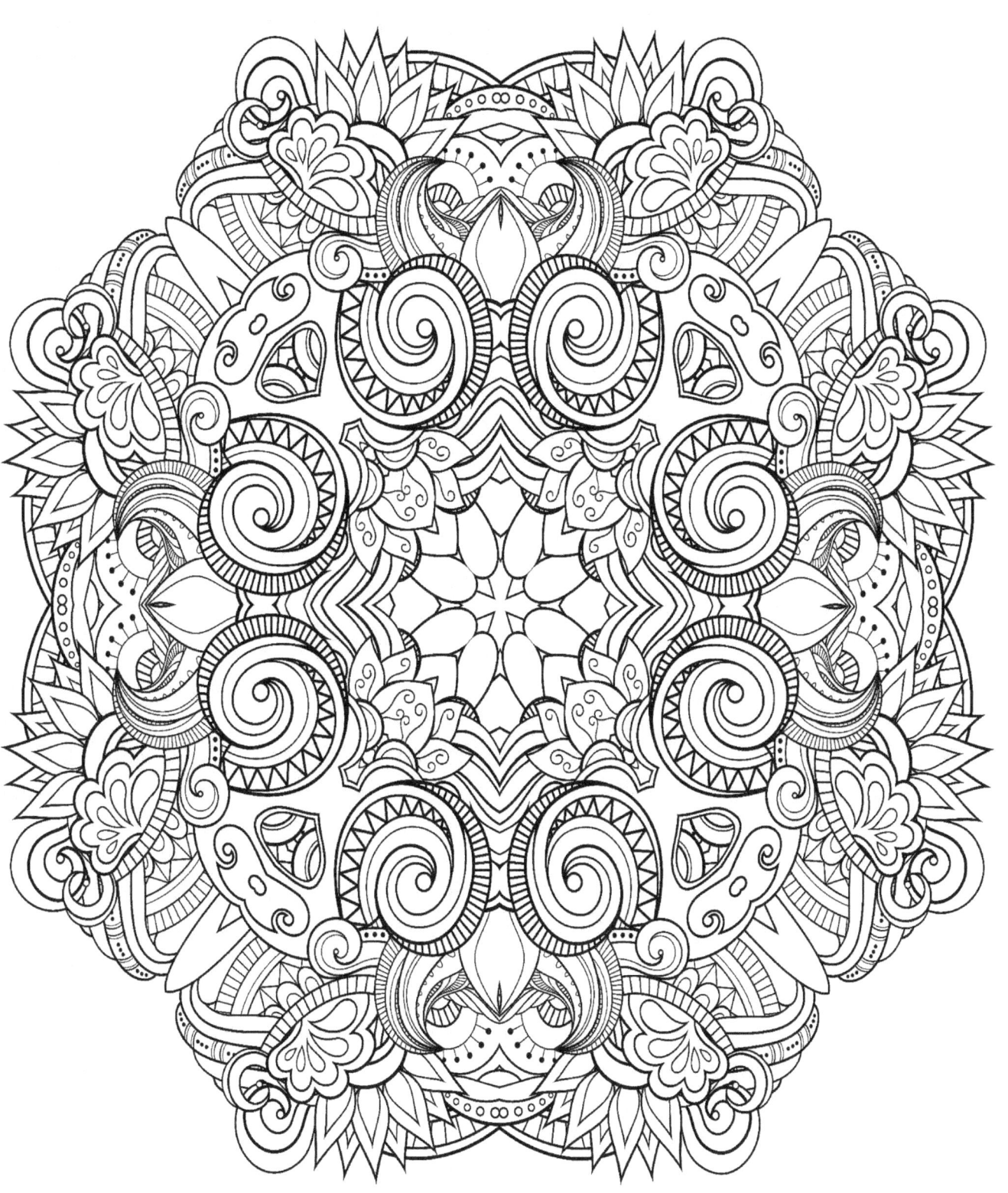

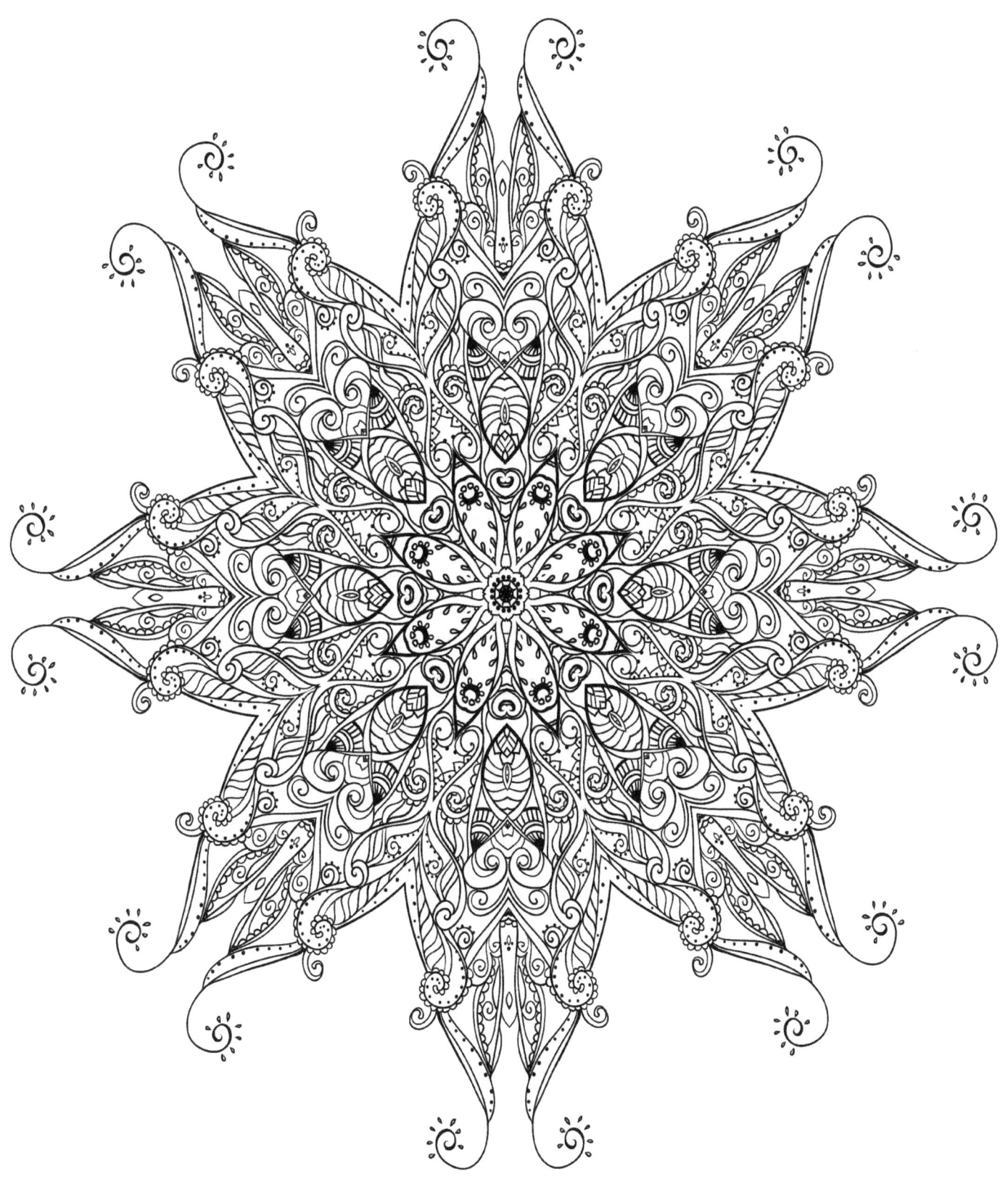

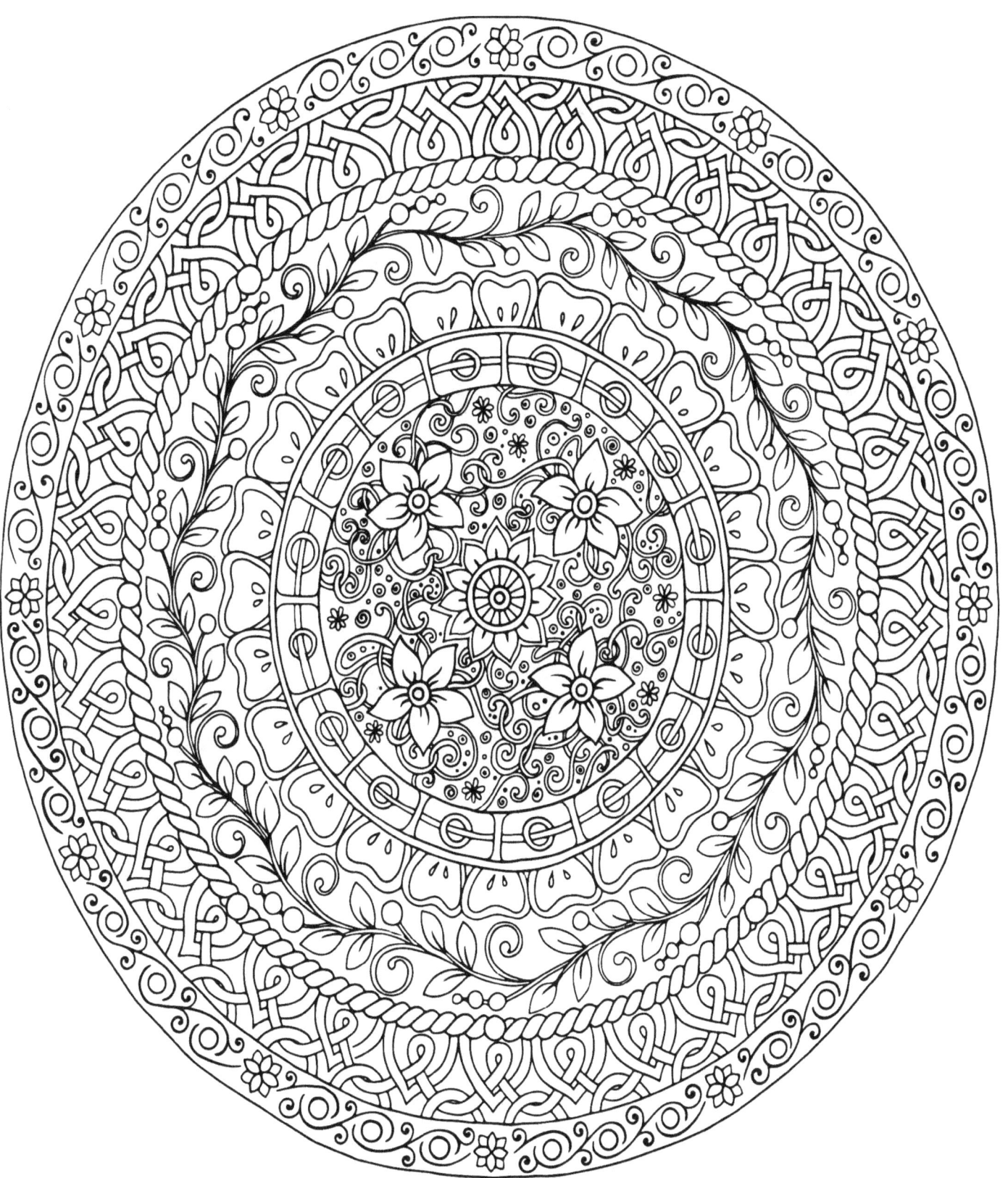

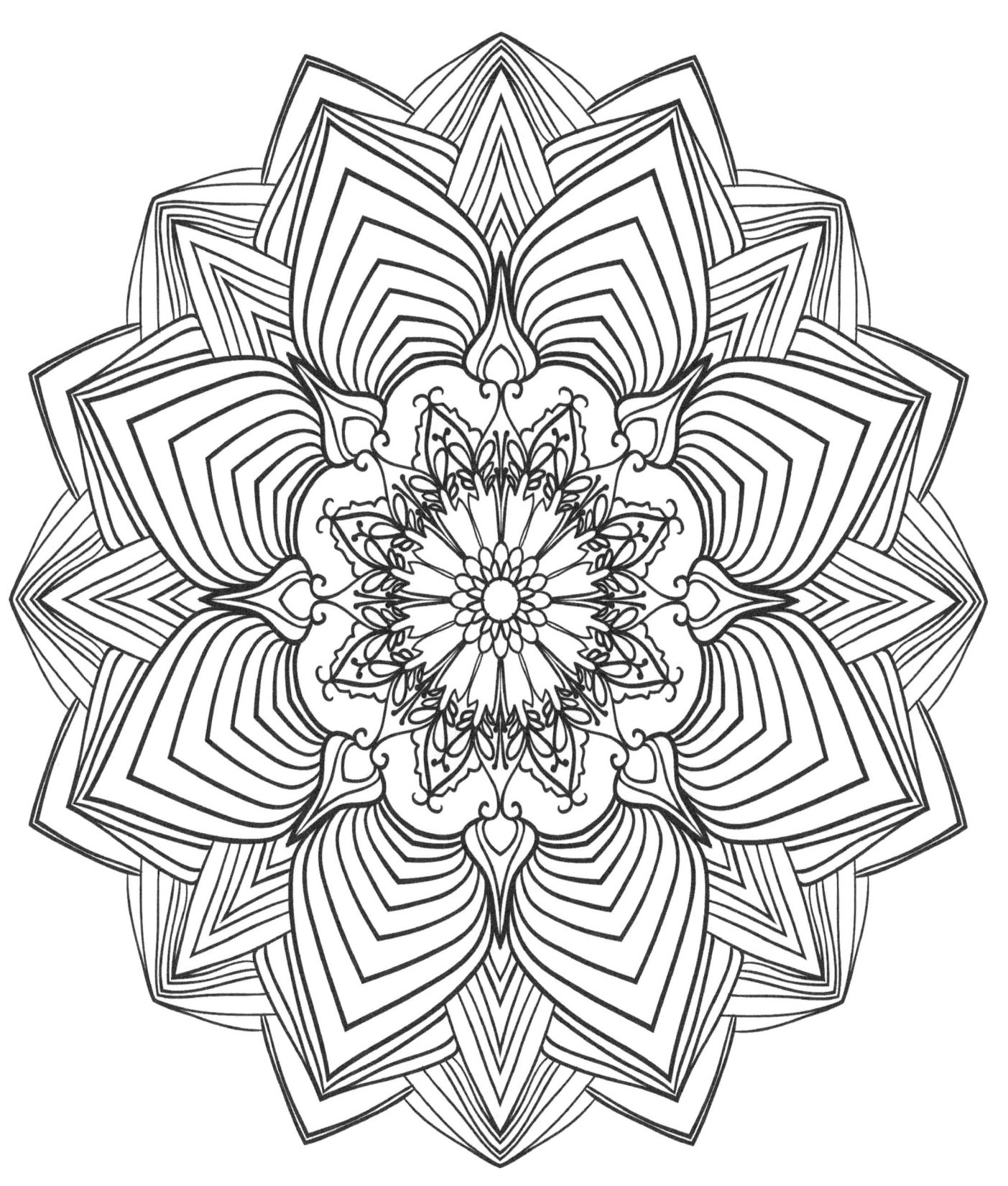

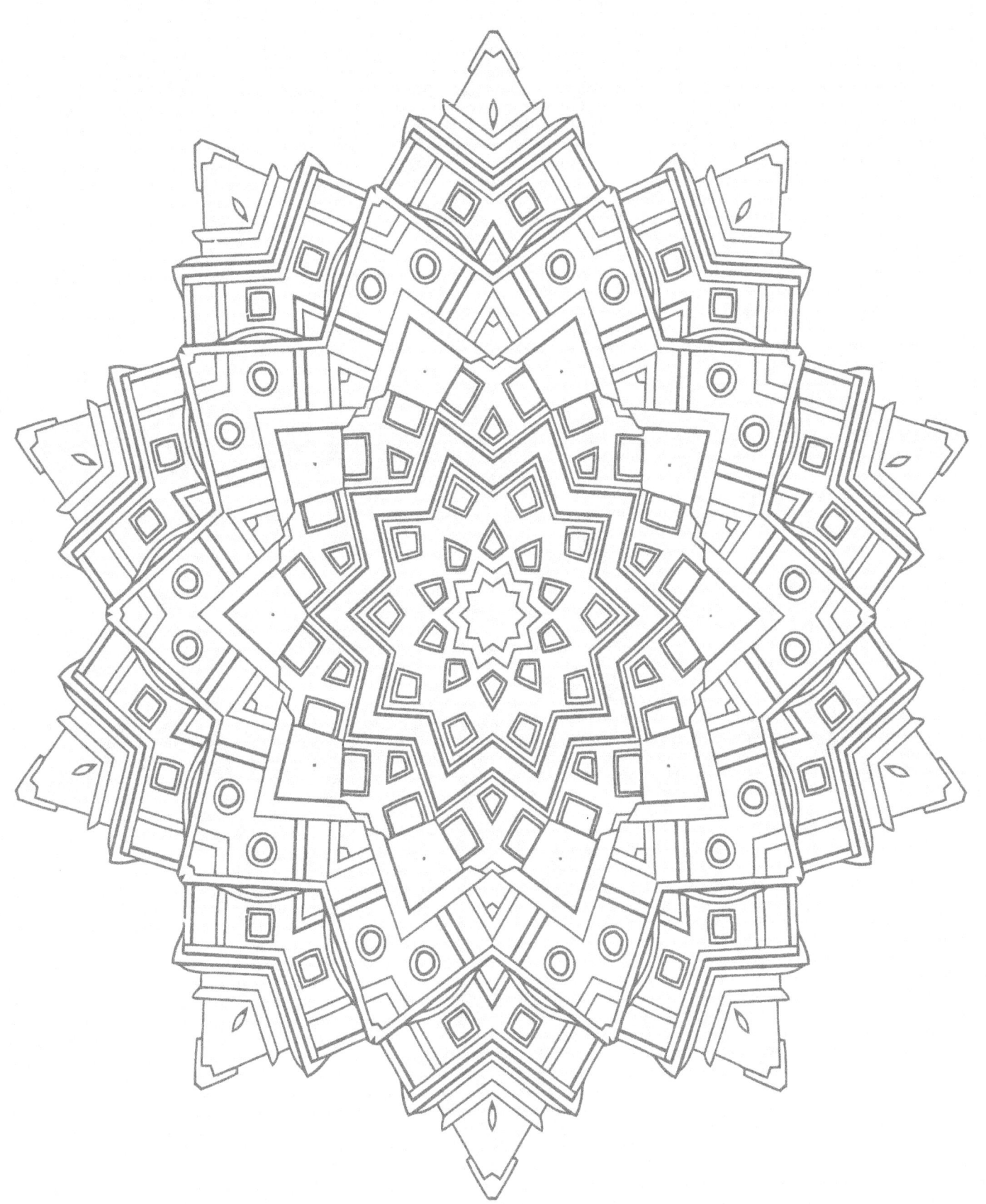

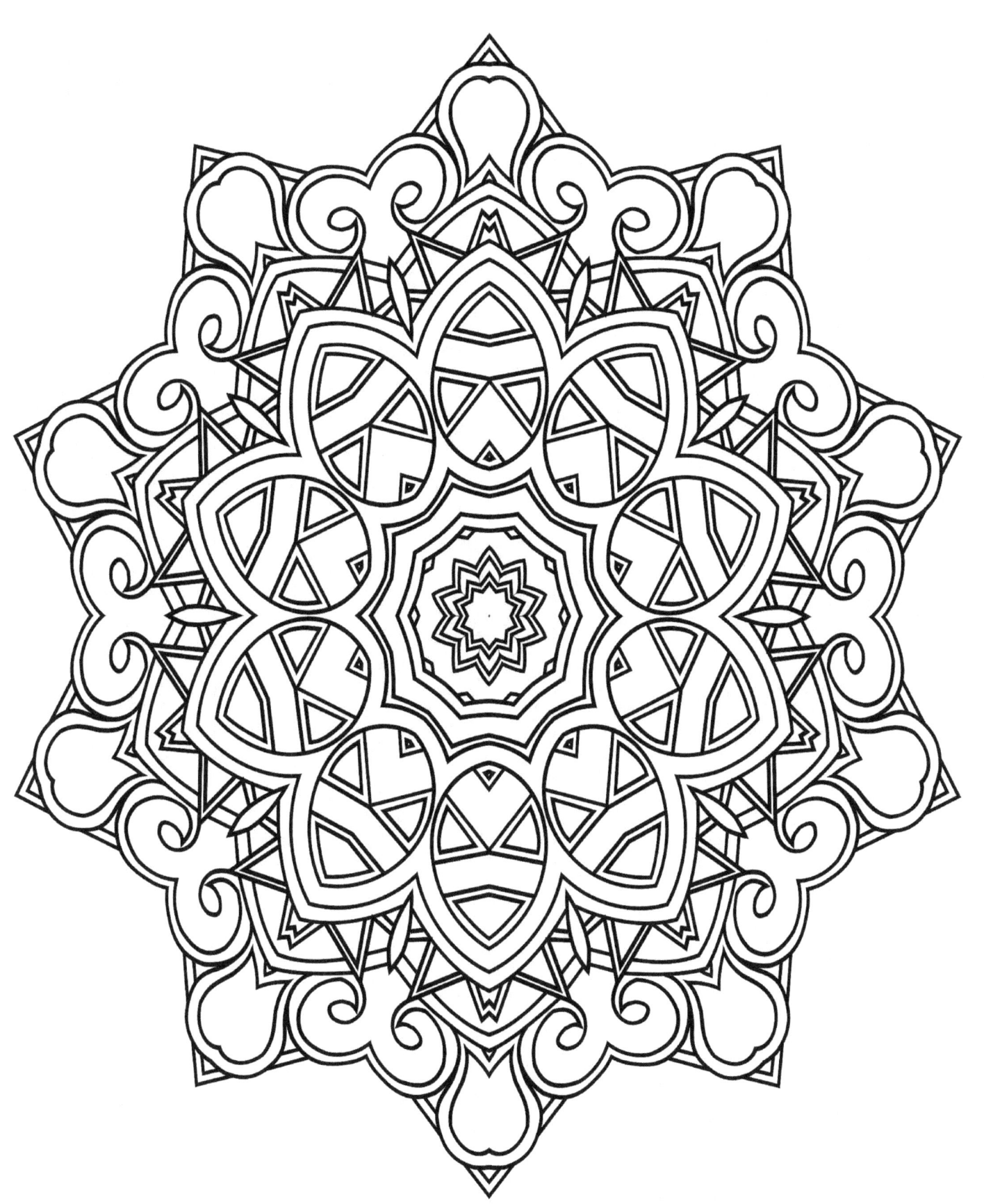

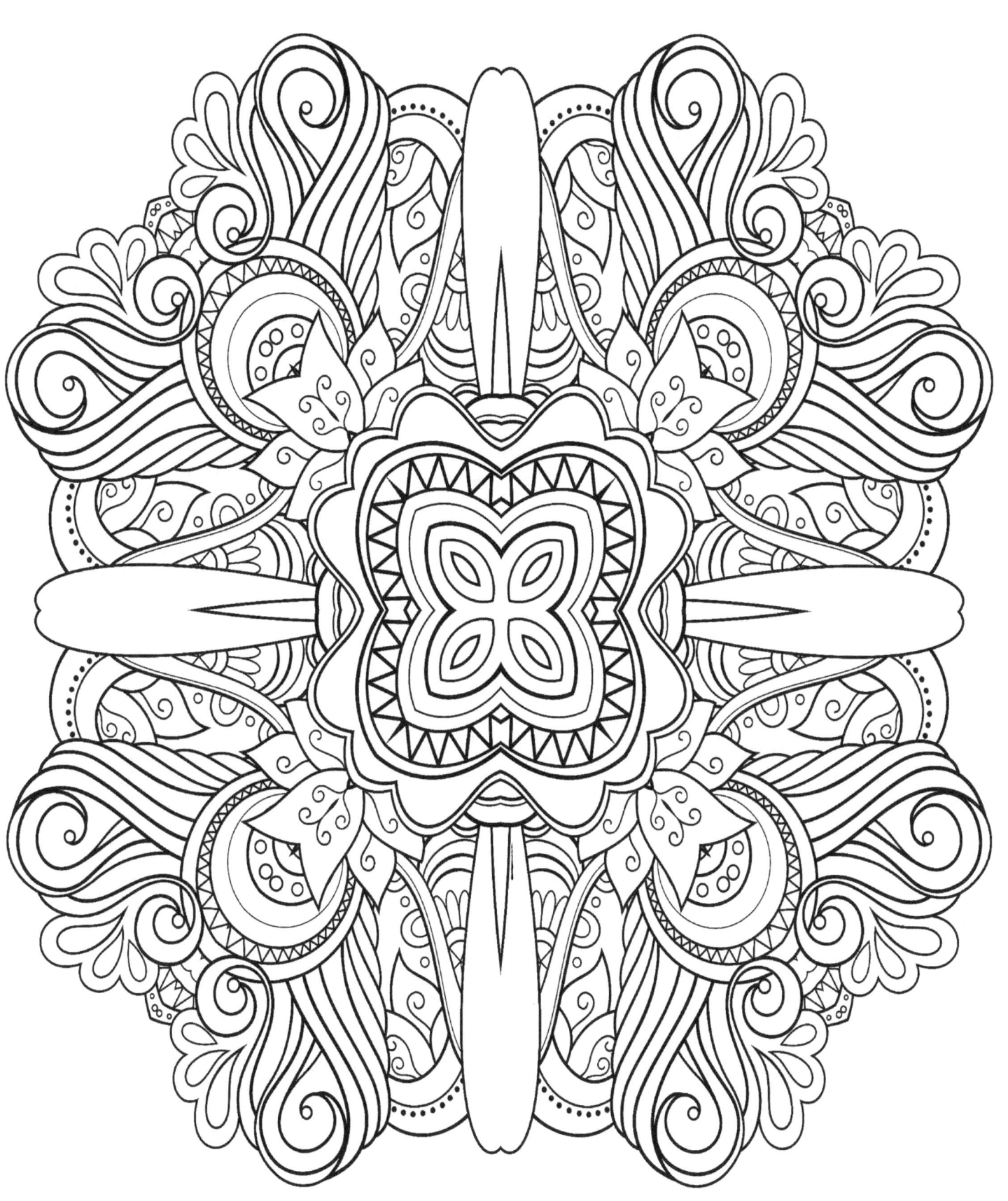

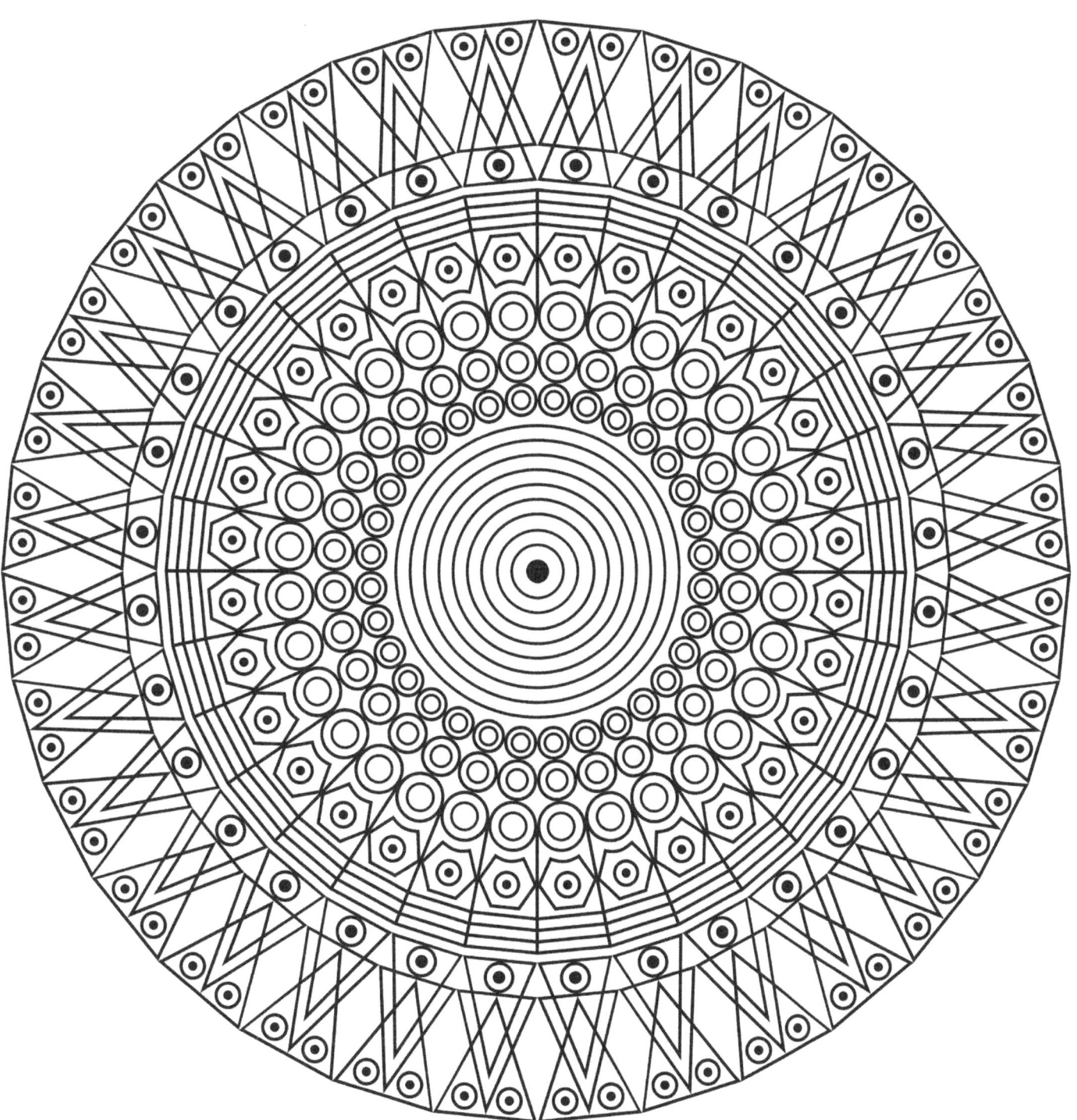

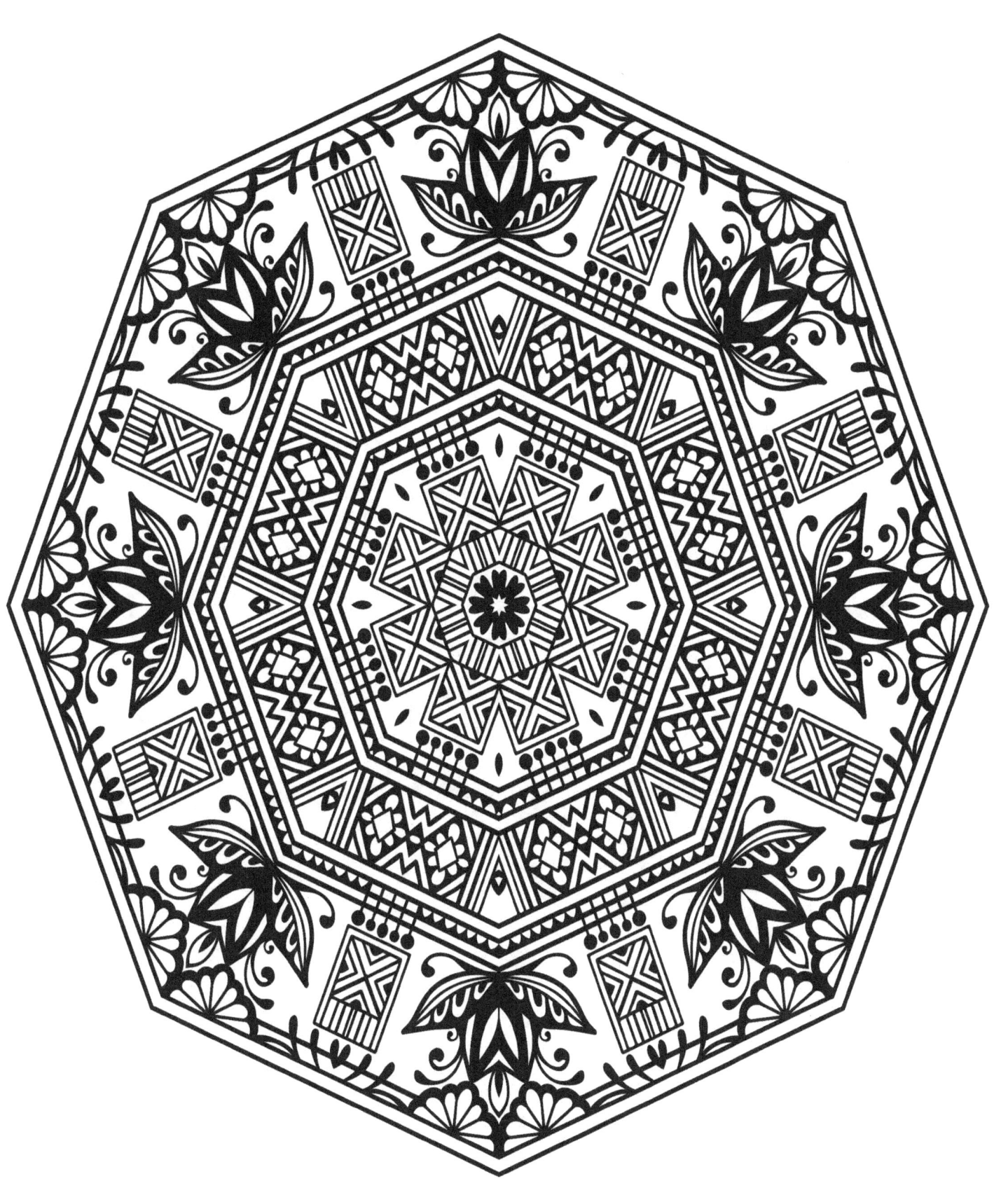

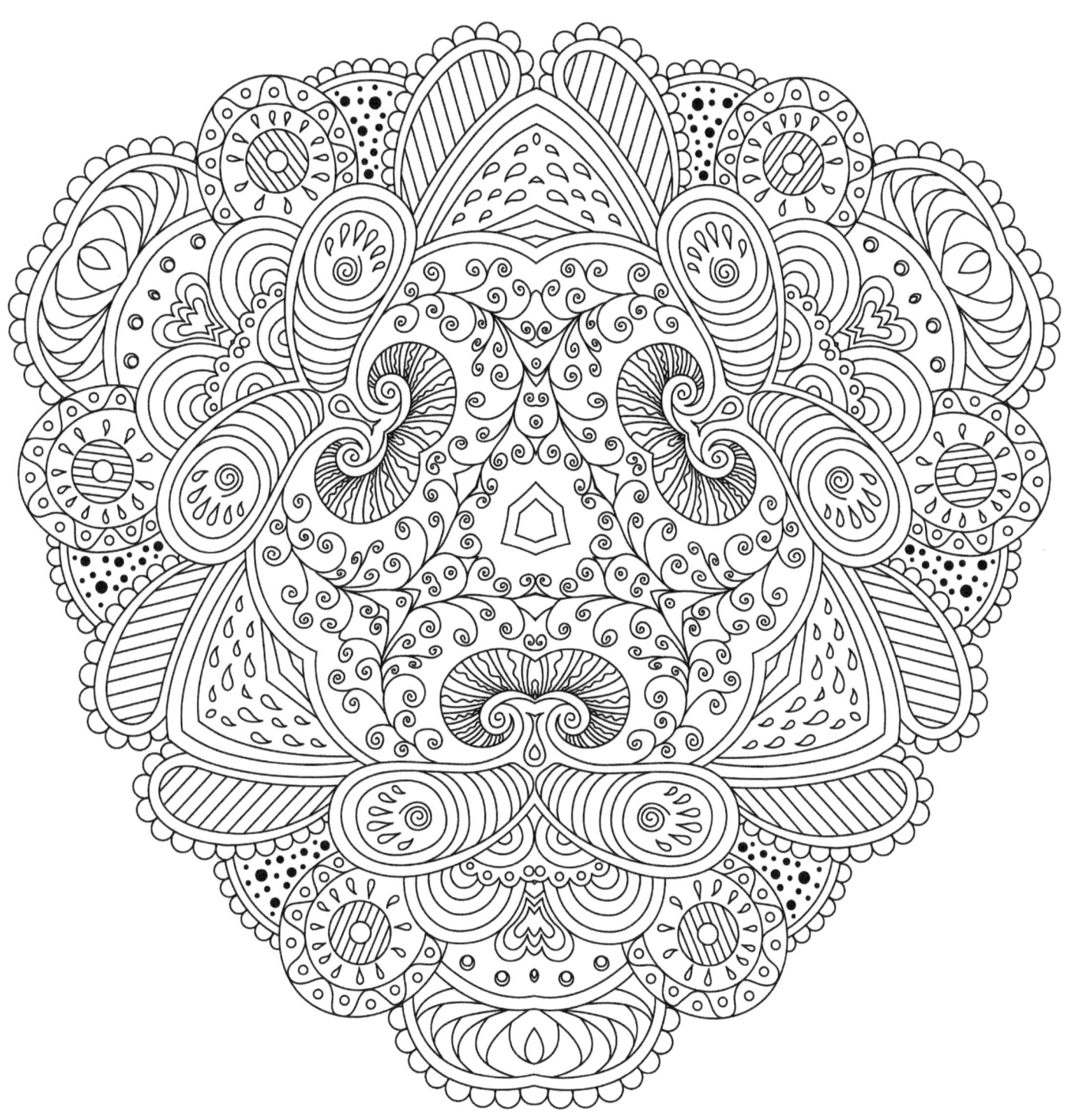

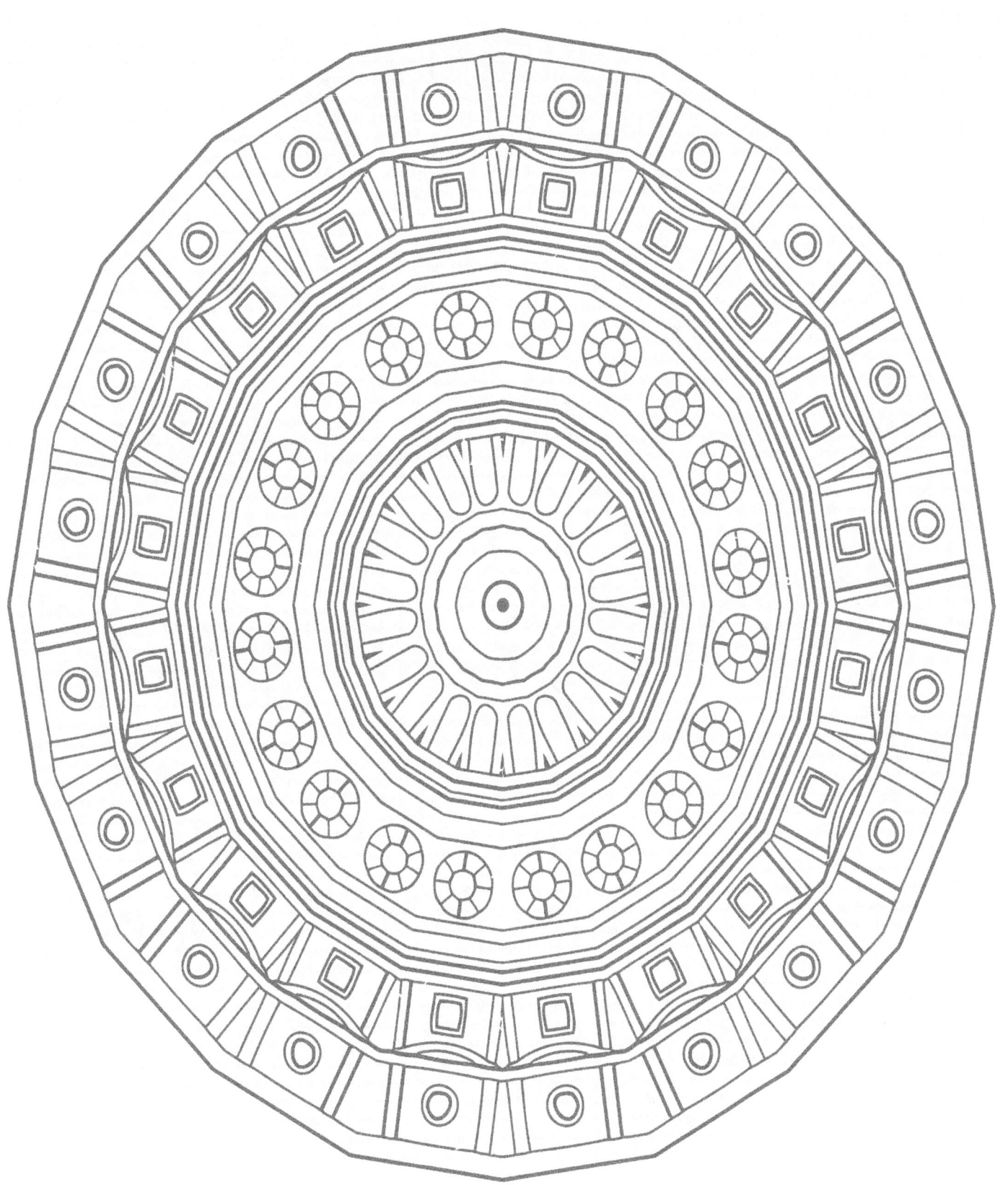

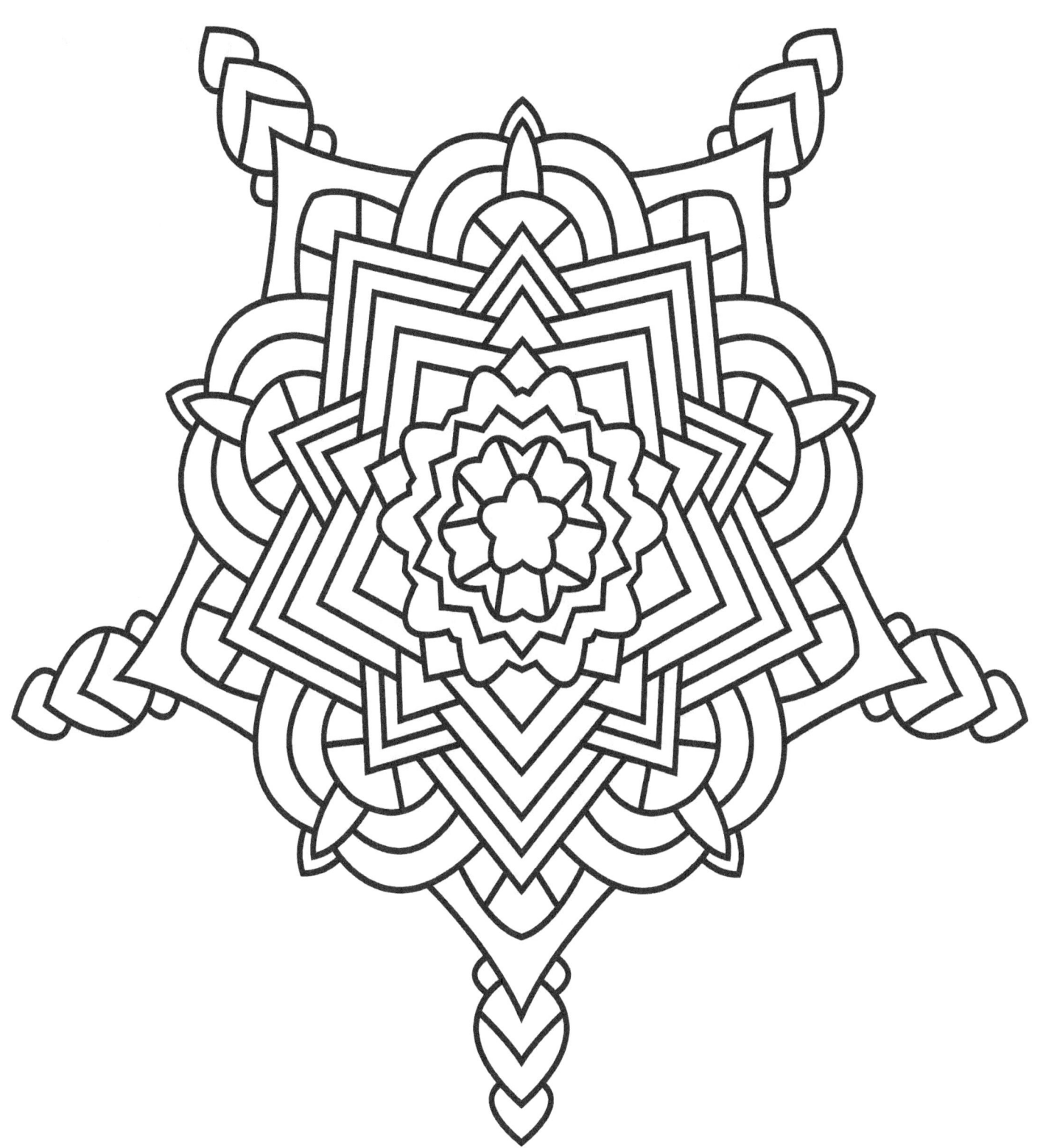

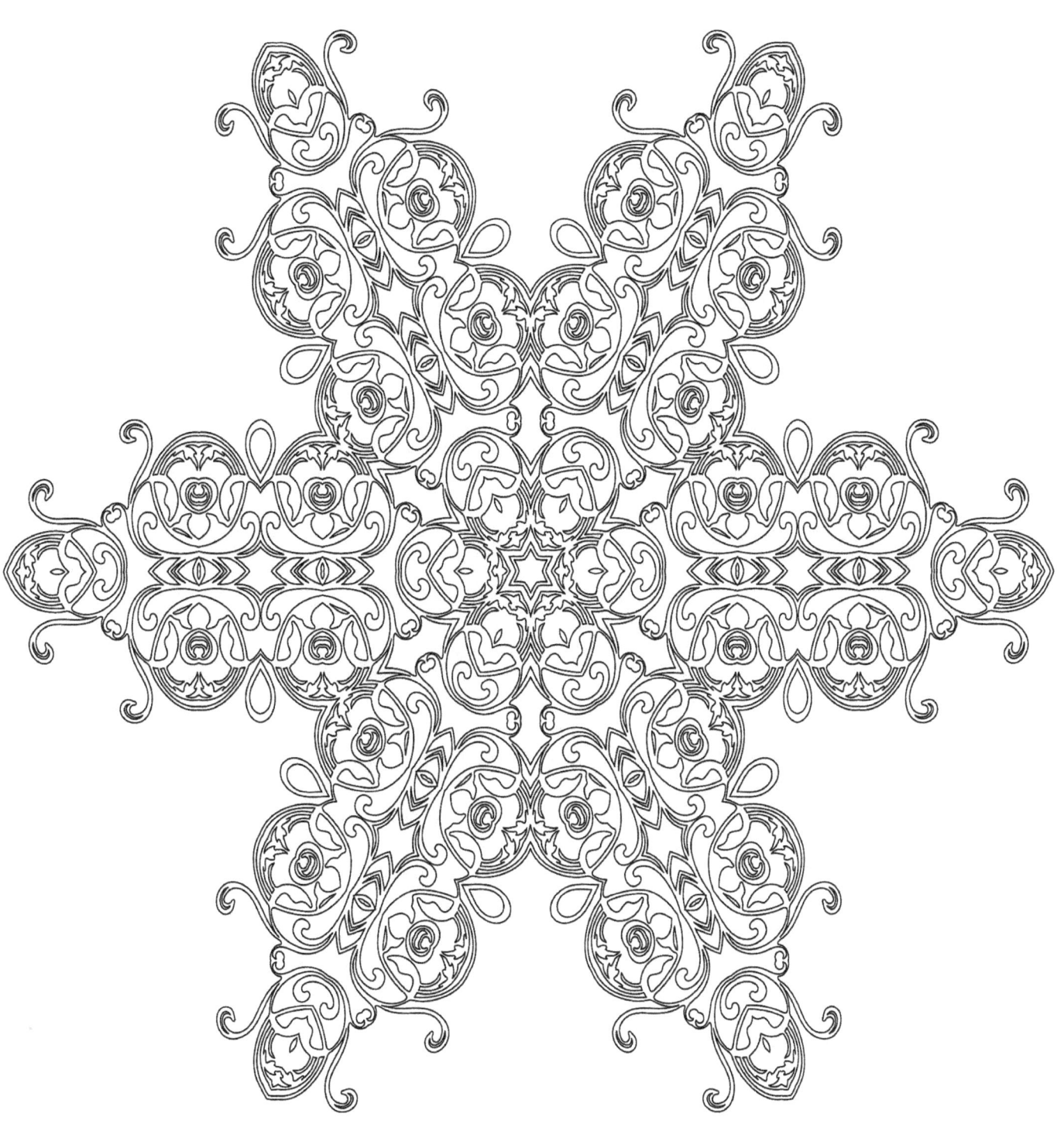

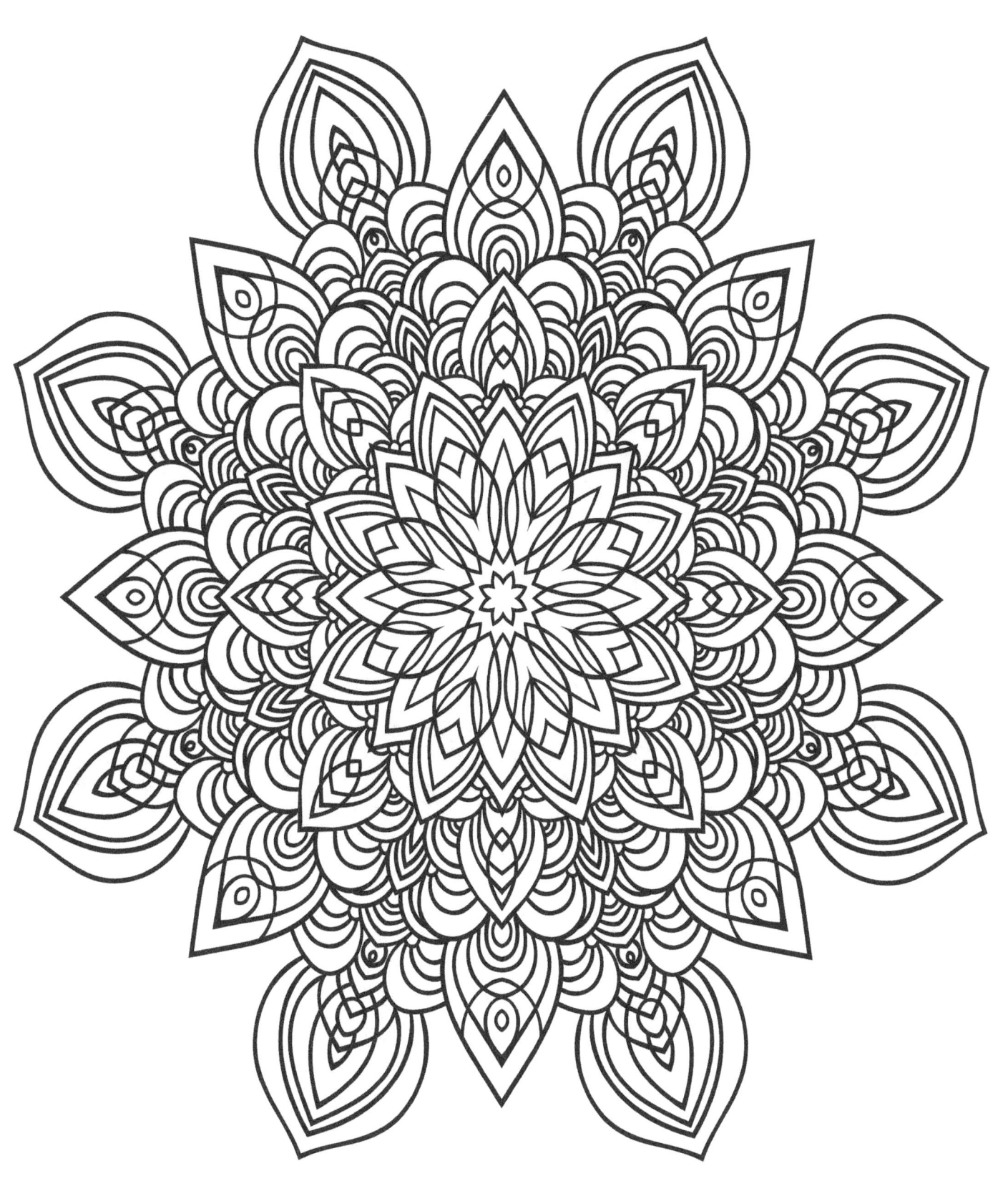

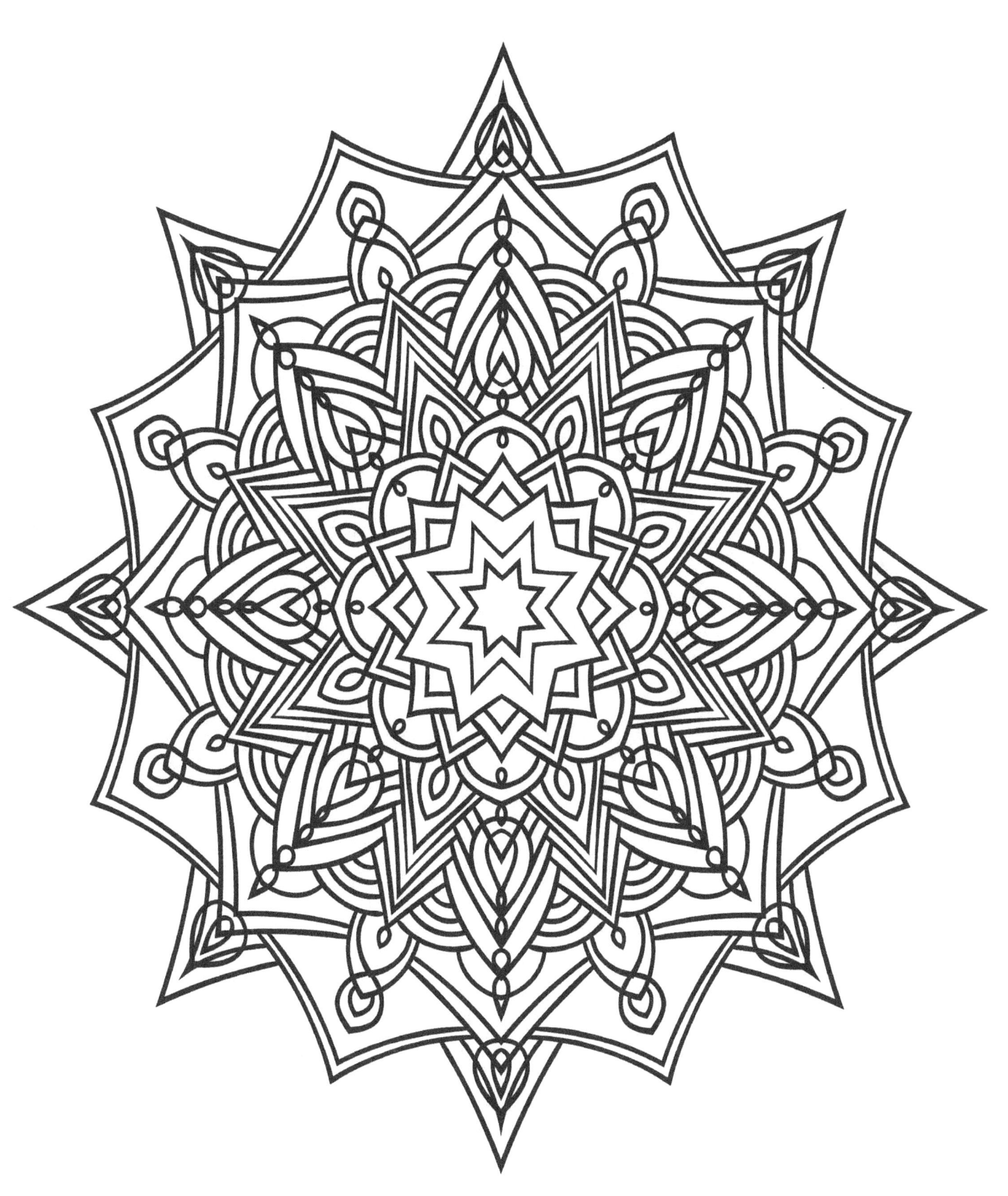

# Be Happy Coloring Books

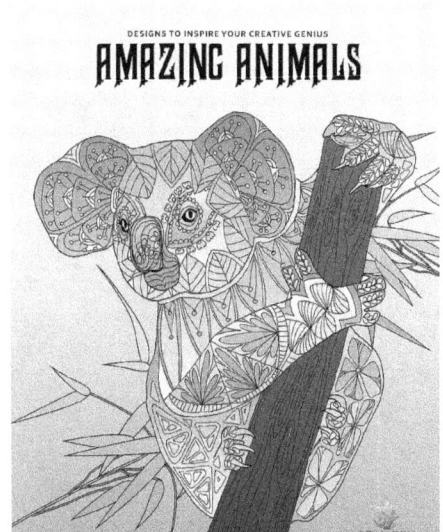

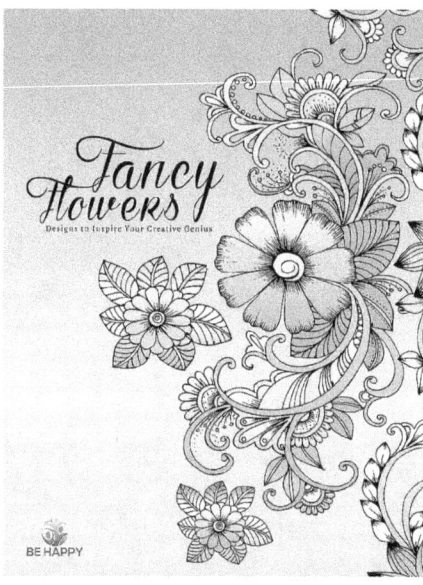

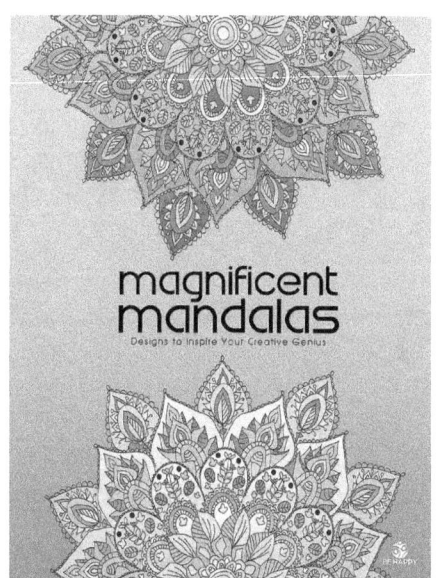

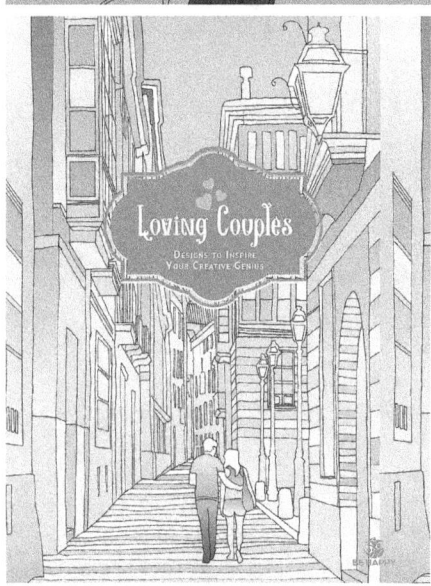

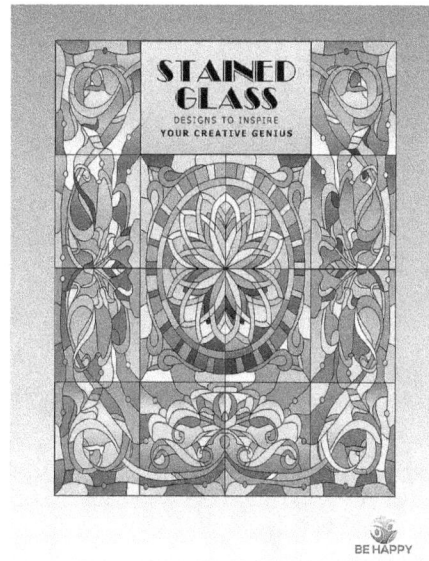

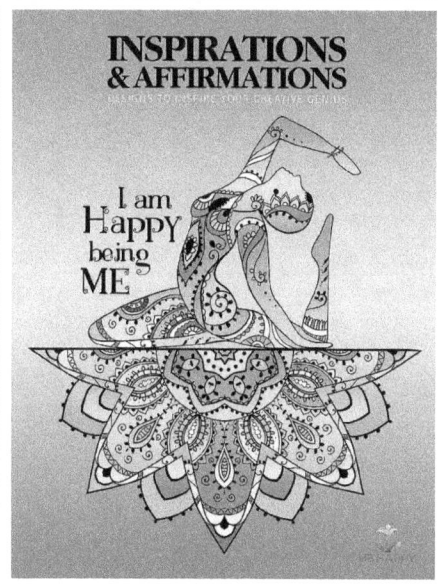

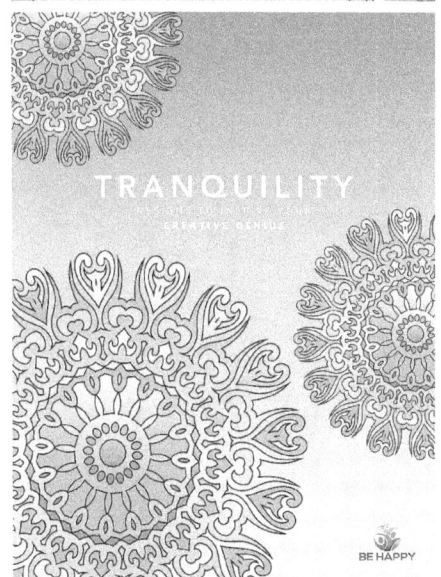

Stay tuned, more coloring books to come.
Our artists are passionately creating
new coloring pages to help inspire
your creative genius.

www.BeHappyColoringBooks.com

www.ingramcontent.com/pod-product-compliance
Lightning Source LLC
Chambersburg PA
CBHW080945170526

45158CB00008B/2384